growing
up
lonely

growing up lonely

disconnection and misconnection in the lives of our children

Edited by J. W. Freiberg, PhD, JD

PROCEEDINGS FROM THE SYMPOSIUM ON CHILDHOOD LONELINESS
"LONELINESS AND THE POWER OF PERMANENCY"
SPONSORED BY THE HOME FOR LITTLE WANDERERS, INC.
THE KENNEDY CENTER, APRIL 2018

PHILIA BOOKS, LTD., BOSTON

Published by Philia Books, Ltd., Boston, MA
www.thelonelinessbook.com

Edited and designed by Girl Friday Productions
www.girlfridayproductions.com

Editorial: Dave Valencia, Michelle Hope, Avi Kool
Cover design: Kathleen Lynch

Cover image credits © Jake Olson

Newspaper extract on pp. xiv–xv from the *New York Times*. © 2018 The New York Times Company. All rights reserved. Used under license.

ISBN (paperback): 978-0-9975899-2-4
ISBN (ebook): 978-0-9975899-3-1

Library of Congress Control Number: 2019912639

growing up lonely

CONTENTS

DEDICATION

The papers presented in this book were first delivered at a symposium held on April 24, 2018, in the stunningly beautiful reproduction of the Senate chambers in the Edward M. Kennedy Institute for the United States Senate, which is located on the Boston waterfront adjacent to the John F. Kennedy Presidential Library. Ex-Governor Deval Patrick was scheduled to give a brief talk to open the symposium, but when urgent business required his attention elsewhere, he sent the following message:

April 23, 2018
I am so sorry that the press of other business will keep me from being with you on Tuesday morning. I hate to miss the chance to thank The Home for Little Wanderers for its two centuries of service to the children and families of the commonwealth, and to honor my friend and erstwhile chief of staff, Joan Wallace-Benjamin, for her two decades of service to The Home as its president, and to congratulate my friend and law school classmate, J. W. ("Terry") Freiberg, for his three decades of service to The Home and to a number of its sister agencies, as their general counsel. And while I have not yet had the pleasure of meeting Dr. Benjamin's successor, Ms. Lesli Suggs, I salute her

on being chosen to take the reins of the country's very first children's social welfare organization to open its doors back in the eighteenth century.

I have never doubted that the human heart yearns for a sense of connectedness, a sense of community. While any given program must meet the basic needs of the children it serves, and any given intervention on behalf of children must respond to immediate crises in their lives, surely the larger meaning of what social and childcare workers aim to do is to reknit the sense that we each have of a stake in our neighbor's dreams and struggles, just as we have in our own. I know you will be talking about the loneliness children and adults alike feel when their sense of community is frayed, and about what can be done in the service of restoring what is lost when this comes to pass.

Have a great symposium.

Deval Patrick
Governor of the Commonwealth of Massachusetts
(2007–2015)

PREFACE
AND A NOTE OF GRATITUDE

THE 2018 SYMPOSIUM ON LONELINESS
IN THE LIVES OF OUR CHILDREN

I have the distinct impression that many, perhaps most, of us can look back on our lives and second-guess key decisions we made that were bad calls. But then there were all those other decisions—all too often made with scant information and questionable logic—that somehow came out just right, and made all the difference.

One such decision for me was when I was contemplating leaving one of Boston's premier law firms for a proffered partnership at a much smaller firm. I was torn, for various reasons, until The Home for Little Wanderers—the nation's oldest and one of Boston's largest children's social service agencies— contacted me to say that if I became associated with the smaller firm with its far more modest fee schedule, it would appoint me its general counsel. This was enough to entice me to make the switch, and never in my work life did I make a better decision. Above and beyond providing nearly thirty years of fascinating law work up until my retirement from the active practice of law, The Home was of a size and level of sophistication where it could take advantage of my double training—and it allowed me, from time to time, to make use of my academic training. More precisely, twice over the years, The Home invited me to organize symposia, the likes of which, to my knowledge, have never been organized by any other children's social service agency anywhere in the United States—ever.

The first symposium took place in May 2005 and was concerned with adolescent sexuality—a critically important but rarely broached topic. Eli Newberger, MD, professor of pediatric medicine at Harvard Medical School, and founder of the Child Protection Team and Family Development Program at Boston Children's Hospital, spoke about the effects of childhood sexual abuse on the development of adolescent character. Bessel van der Kolk, MD, professor of psychiatry at Boston University, and medical director of the Trauma Center, gave an enlightening talk about how he and his colleagues had learned that trauma victims, with particular reference to childhood sexual abuse victims, cannot be successfully treated with purely verbal talk therapy. This, he explained, is because children's memories of sexualized trauma involve the limbic system: these frightening memories are stored somatically, in the brain stem, not in the forebrain like a memorized list. They are stored as feelings, he told us, not ideas, so the therapy for adolescents with traumatic memories from earlier sexual abuse must involve corporal treatment modalities along with talk therapy.

In the afternoon, Dr. Ann Burgess, professor of psychiatric/mental health nursing at Boston College and one of the world's foremost authorities on why children so often compulsively reenact past traumatic events, explained how impermanency in a child's home life all too often later develops into an inability to form and secure a safe home in their adult life. Then, Bronwyn Mayden, executive director of the Campaign for Our Children, relayed her research on the effects of today's highly sexualized media content on the onset of sexuality in our children, and on the sexual practices of today's adolescents. Finally, I delivered a paper on how children's social service agencies can deal with the conflict between the realities of the earlier onset of sexuality in today's teenagers and the regulatory restraints with which the agencies must comply that ban all touching—and certainly all sexuality—in residential treatment settings.

More recently, in the early summer of 2017, Joan Wallace-Benjamin, PhD, then the outgoing president of The Home, asked me to present my story "The Loneliest Boy"—which is reprinted in this volume—to The Home's three dozen program directors and key administrative personnel. The conversation at the presentation was so vibrant, and the model I presented was so supportive of The Home's then newly launched efforts to promote "permanency planning" for each and every residential and outpatient child The Home works with, that the collective group present that day asked me to organize another full-scale symposium. The new symposium was to be based on my story, "The Loneliest Boy," and was to explore the ever-more-prevalent chronic loneliness exhibited by The Home's young clients. It was left up to me to invite other speakers whose work I found to be at the cutting edge of understanding and treating the desperate feeling of being disconnected and alone—a feeling that more and more children were reporting to The Home's clinicians in their counseling sessions. What a fabulous opportunity—and what an awesome responsibility. I am grateful to The Home from the bottom of my heart.

And so, almost a year later, the symposium "Loneliness and the Power of Permanency" was held on a stunningly clear day at the Edward M. Kennedy Institute for the United States Senate. The beautifully reproduced copy of the United States Senate chamber where the symposium took place is on the grounds of the John F. Kennedy Presidential Library and Museum—on the waterfront of Boston's outer harbor. President Kennedy's sailboat, the Victura, still sits up on dry land by the library, waiting patiently, poignantly, for its skipper to return.

Even better than the venue, however, were the participants. With only a score of exceptions, the attendees were hundreds of mental health clinicians who sought both the training in the content of the talks and also the continuing-education credits these professionals needed to meet their requirements for licensure renewal. These clinicians work on a daily basis with abused and traumatized children in outpatient and residential settings throughout the Commonwealth of Massachusetts, so it was truly our honor, as speakers, to address such a knowledgeable audience. Taking a conservative guess at the years of experience they had on average, and multiplying by the number of clinicians in attendance, we on the podium were humbled at the prospect of presenting our thoughts on children and loneliness to an audience with more than five thousand years—five thousand years—of collective practical, real-world clinical experience treating children with issues that so often included feeling inadequately connected—and thereby, lonely, unprotected, and unsafe.

The Loneliness of Our Times

The *New York Times* published an article on January 17, 2018, stating:

> LONDON—Since Britain voted to leave the European Union more than a year ago, Europeans have mockingly said that the decision will result in an isolated, lonely island nation.
>
> But Britain, in fact, already has a serious problem with loneliness, research has found.

> More than nine million people in the country often or always feel lonely, according to a 2017 report published by the Jo Cox Commission on Loneliness.
>
> The issue prompted Prime Minister Theresa May on Wednesday to appoint a minister for loneliness.
>
> "For far too many people, loneliness is the sad reality of modern life," Mrs. May said in a statement.

The chronic loneliness to which the British prime minister is referring didn't exist until recent years, except, one would assume, in isolated individuals. When life was local, when one was surrounded throughout one's life by family and childhood friends, when most people lived their entire lives in the community into which they were born—whether that be in a village or in a small town, or even in an ethnically defined communitylike neighborhood of yesteryear's larger cities—everyone knew everyone else. There simply wasn't enough social space to grow lonely in.

Jacqueline Olds, MD, and Richard S. Schwartz, MD, both associate clinical professors of psychiatry at Harvard Medical School, each of whom has contributed a paper to this volume, were among the first psychiatrists to recognize the ever-increasing presence of chronic loneliness and the fact that social isolation has become a major public health crisis. Their groundbreaking book *Overcoming Loneliness in Everyday Life* was the first major work to explore the appearance in everyday life of the new loneliness, and the terrible toll it takes on the mental health of those afflicted. Their more recent work in this sphere, *The Lonely American: Drifting Apart in the Twenty-first Century,* was among the earliest studies to tie this new loneliness to the changing demographics of contemporary urban life: they pointed out how well over a third of adult households were now single-person households. Olds and Schwartz perceived and described how certain deeply embedded socioeconomic structures in modern-day life have the side effect of generating the increasingly prevalent chronic loneliness of our era, and they contrasted the recent appearance of this systemically induced loneliness with past times, when "individualism" was an ideology about self-reliance and not yet a description of lives spent eating microwaved meals on a folding table in front of a television set—alone.

Perhaps even more ominously, structurally determined chronic loneliness has now spread to our children. Amy Banks, MD, director of advanced training at the Jean Baker Miller Training Institute for relational-cultural theory and a senior scholar at the Wellesley Centers for Women at Wellesley College, the fourth contributor to this volume, informs us that the absence—or even the inadequacy—of healthy connections in the home and neighborhood lives of our children has become a significant contributing factor to the ever-growing presence of adult chronic loneliness. Dr. Banks provides an analysis of the physiology of loneliness: how our disconnected children *fail to fully develop the neural pathways in their brains* they will need as adults to successfully connect with others in the ways and to the extent that their mental health will require. She makes this point succinctly and convincingly in the paper she has contributed to this edited volume, but you can find a far more extensive treatment of the topic in the book she authored with Leigh Ann Hirschman, *Wired to Connect: The Surprising Link Between Brain Science and Strong, Healthy Relationships.*

My own modest efforts to understand the scourge of chronic loneliness that degrades the mental health of so many children in our era consists of trying to understand how a child can be propelled into chronic loneliness either by disconnection (isolation) or by misconnection (defective linkages). "The Loneliest Boy" story that opens this collection is a reprint of a case study found in my recent book, *Four Seasons of Loneliness: A Lawyer's Case Stories.* This story about the life of an ever-more-disconnected boy attempts to understand and explicate how the incest to which he was subjected in his family home set him up to repeat an incestuous relationship on his own initiative, which, in turn, doomed him to a life of chronic loneliness. I should mention that "The Loneliest Boy" was e-mailed to each entrant who registered to attend the 2018 symposium, which gave everyone present that day some common ground for discussion purposes. As you might imagine, this greatly enlivened and energized the extended question-and-answer portion at the end of the day. Once again, I have placed "The Loneliest Boy" first in this collection—based on the same logic, as several of the other contributors' papers make reference to it.

My second contribution concludes this volume. "Growing Up Lonely: Disconnection and Misconnection in the Lives of Our Children" tells the stories of five children whom I met in my law practice. All of these children were at great risk of experiencing chronic loneliness not because they were physically isolated in life, but because they were *misconnected* to the significant adults in their everyday lives. The analytical model I propose in this essay is discussed in considerably greater depth in my soon-to-be-published book, *Surrounded by Others and Yet So Alone.*

J. W. Freiberg, PhD, JD
Boston
Midsummer Eve, 2019

I

The Loneliest Boy

J.W. FREIBERG, PHD, JD

"Hi, Terry. Susan Sears here. Am I going to lose my house?" These were the first words I heard about a lawsuit that would stretch over three years and teach me more about loneliness than I ever wanted to learn. Ten minutes earlier my client had been served lawsuit papers, as she put it, "by the biggest goddamn sheriff I've ever seen. And he was out to scare me. Why would he do that?" Once I had calmed her down to the point where she could read me the heading to the lawsuit papers, I learned that she had indeed been sued, as had the small adoption agency she had run for over twenty years.

But allow me to step back a moment and explain how I got to one end of the phone line and Susan got to the other. In the fall of 1971, I became an assistant professor of sociology at Boston University, where I principally taught courses in social psychology. I was fascinated by the nature of the linkage between mind and society, how our perceptions and thoughts are colored and, to some extent, even structured by the era and social circumstances in which we live. I was ecstatic about my academic life in vibrant Boston, save for one problem: Boston University had an autocratic president who was so odious that he managed to provoke nearly the entire faculty to go on strike in 1975. I quickly became one of the leaders of the strike, and along with the other organizers, I appeared before the board of trustees—and the president—to present the junior faculty's view as to why his contract should not be renewed. As it turned out, the trustees determined to indeed renew the president's contract, and lo and behold, when my candidature for tenure came across his desk in 1978, it was *my* contract that was not renewed. Although a year later I was actually awarded tenure, I had in the interim applied to and been accepted to Harvard Law School, and since the problematic president was willing to pay my tuition in exchange for my resignation, off I went in 1980 to begin an entirely new career.

Little did I know that once I had learned the basics of practicing law, I would be almost immediately typecast as the attorney to whom cases and clients involving any and all sundry psychological issues should be sent. I had envisioned myself as a constitutional lawyer arguing great legal theories before the Supreme Court. But no, that was not to be the case. On the contrary, I practiced law "in the trenches," as the saying goes. And while the nature of my practice meant that neither fame nor fortune would come my way, it also meant that I would, in effect, be doing social psychological research through practicing law. It was only in retirement, however, that I took the time to write about the observations I had made daily for more than thirty years.

So back to my client Susan Sears. She had retained my general counsel services about five years before this lawsuit because she had heard about my previous career, my sympathetic ear for social service agencies, and—not unimportantly—my modest fee schedule. I asked her to fax over the lawsuit documents, relax with a cup of tea, and give me an hour to read over the papers.

I could see almost at once that the complaint and its collateral documents were well drafted. That's actually a good thing: quality counsel on the plaintiff's side of a personal injury lawsuit greatly increases the odds of a timely resolution. That being said, the complaint was sparsely written, and about all I could discern from the papers was that Susan and her agency were being blamed for a failed adoption that had shattered the adoptive home, traumatizing everybody in the family—adults and children alike. Since children were involved, the adoptive parents were identified as John and Jane Doe, their adoptive daughter was called Ashley Doe, and their preadoptive foster son—Ashley's biological brother—was dubbed Seth Doe. One thing, however, was abundantly clear: the plaintiffs were seeking massive monetary damages.

It was also obvious that the plaintiffs had brought a "shotgun" lawsuit; that is, they were suing anybody and everybody involved in any way with the failed adoptive placement. Additional defendants included the Massachusetts Department of Social Services (DSS) and about a dozen psychiatrists and psychologists. The DSS was accused of negligently managing the adoptive placement, while the mental health professionals, all of whom had treated the two adoptive children at different times after their removal from their birth family, were accused of negligence in failing to warn the adoptive parents about how the children might behave once they were placed.

The multiparty nature of the lawsuit meant two things to me: first, it was unlikely to settle quickly, and second, it was going to cost a small fortune to defend. I called Sears back.

"There's good news," I began, "and bad news. The good news is, you don't need to worry about your house. The nature of the claims means that it will certainly be covered by your agency's professional liability insurance policy, and I reviewed that policy last spring, I know for a fact that it is in full force and effect. And by the way, your policy has no deductible, so neither the agency nor any of you will have to pay a penny out of pocket, so you can relax."

"Okay, great." She paused. "Wait a minute. You said there's bad news too."

"The bad news is that this kind of lawsuit is likely to drag on for two or three years."

"Years! How do we handle this mess and make a living? There's only three of us." I could hear distress in her voice.

For the next half hour, I walked Sears through what it means—in practical terms—to be sued. I explained how the legal discovery process works and told her that, absent a settlement, the case would not proceed to trial for at least three years.

"You'll be our attorney on this, won't you?" Sears pleaded.

"That's up to your insurance company," I explained. "But by all odds, they'll agree to that. Even if they don't, I can be involved as the agency's general counsel. One way or another, I'm going to hold your hand throughout this entire process."

"Thank you, thank you, Terry," she said with real emotion in her voice, audibly exhaling into the phone. I could tell she was tearing up.

*

Sure enough, when I called the agency's insurer, the company's senior claim agent, Rhonda Wilkins, gave me the case to defend. She knew from past cases we had done together that my training in social psychology would be useful, especially because this case would involve depositions of more than a score of mental health professionals, not to mention our need to locate and work with a forensic psychiatrist to serve as our expert witness.

The plaintiffs' attorney was Jeff O'Toole. He and I had once served together on a Massachusetts Bar Association committee, and I had formed the impression that he was a reasonably classy guy, especially for someone who practiced plaintiff-side personal injury law. Working with him, I thought, would be far better than what I could have drawn: a back-of-the-yellow-pages ambulance chaser. But reaching him was another matter. I called, but it took O'Toole more than a week to get back to me. Not a promising start.

In the meantime, Sears sent me three boxes' worth of the agency's case records from the Doe adoptive placement. They arrived on the Friday before a three-day weekend in the still-chilly early spring. I took the documents home, set up a card table in front of my living room fireplace, and spent all three of those days reading the record from front to back. There were five fireplaces in our old Civil War–era house, and we used them far too seldom in the rush of modern life. It was delightful to take the opportunity to sit by one for once. My son was about four years old at the time, and he essentially spent the entire three days playing under the table by my feet, enjoying both his fort, as he called it, and the wonderful warmth thrown off by the fire. He was just old enough to help put on the occasional new log, and as I interrupted my reading from time to time to join him under the table, I couldn't help but reflect on how much of one's life is determined by the happenstance of birth. Seth Doe and my boy were born into circumstances as different as could be: Seth's life chances were doomed before he could walk or talk, and there was nothing he could do about it. This, if I remember correctly from college English class, is the technical definition of a tragic flaw: when one's downfall and destruction are predetermined by an ineradicable flaw.

At the time I read the *Doe* case record, I was serving as general counsel to half a dozen children's social service agencies, and in this capacity, I worked closely with the Massachusetts

DSS. Accordingly, I had encountered some extreme and deeply disturbing cases involving the sexual abuse of children. But none of this adequately prepared me for the *Doe* case. I was horrified by what I read in the massive written record.

The two children involved had been raised by a young single mother, and all three of them lived in the home of the children's grandmother and step-grandfather, as did the two siblings of the mother. The family rented a humble house in a town northwest of Boston, and they appeared perfectly normal to the neighbors. The children presented and behaved well in school and in the community, and the adults were polite and accepted in the neighborhood. Teacher and guidance counselor notations that I read in the record drew the same conclusions. All of them consistently indicated that the children were appropriate with their classmates, polite with adults, and diligent in their schoolwork. Other documentation showed that they played well with other children and that their performance on tests and homework was entirely acceptable. Ashley was consistently a strong B student, and Seth's grades averaged out to A–. The school nurse's report was no different: it stated that the children seemed properly fed and exhibited no health or dental problems.

Behind this façade, however, was a home life as abnormal as any of us who worked on the case had ever encountered. The step-grandfather turned out to be, in the words of the chief counsel of the commonwealth's DSS, "one of the most sexually abusive offenders on record in Massachusetts." He not only had sexual relations with his wife, but also with all three of her children—two daughters and one son. Moreover, he had sired the two Doe children by one of his stepdaughters, so he was both their step-grandfather and their father. Still more shocking, he sexually abused these children from the time they were toddlers. The grandmother was also sexually active with all of her children and involved in group sex practices with the toddlers. The young mother of the two children was no different: she likewise engaged in group sex with her siblings in various combinations. So far as I could tell, there were simply no sexual boundaries whatsoever in the children's biological home.

But by far the most peculiar thing about the household (and this may well be as hard for you to accept as it was for me and the ten additional attorneys who would soon be working on the case) was that, although there was unparalleled sexual exploitation of the young adults and constant sexual abuse of the two small children, in every other sphere of life, the family consistently exhibited nurturing and loving concern for each other's welfare. That, obviously, is why the children presented as well in public as they did. Among the score of legal and mental health professionals who worked on the *Doe* case, there were many hundreds of years of collective experience. And yet not one of us had *ever* seen or even heard of this fact pattern (as lawyers call the circumstances of a case) before. On the contrary, in the hundreds of cases involving sexually abused children with which we had collectively dealt, there had always also been physical or psychological abuse—often both. At the very least, children with sexually abusive home lives are typically threatened and frightened into silence: they're told that if they disclose to anyone what goes on at home, they will be permanently taken away from their family. Instilling this fear of separation in a young child is in and of itself psychologically abusive, and it's common to learn that such children are often also threatened with violence if they disclose the family's hidden secrets. But from what I could discern in a first reading of the voluminous Doe record, the method used by the children's family to achieve secrecy and mask their home life was unlike any other I had ever experienced. It was pretty clearly not based on threats.

At some point, I needed a break from reading the enormous and depressing record. I started sifting through the folders, looking for a snapshot, a Polaroid, or a photo of any kind. When I eventually found one in practically the last file I looked in, it absolutely startled me. These were no ordinary children. They were a matched set of stunningly beautiful, blond, blue-eyed kids with big smiles and perfectly straight, white teeth. They looked to be about eight and six years old in the photo, which seemed to have been taken at a playground or park; there was a slide and a swing visible beyond them. One thing seemed certain: the children clearly loved whoever took the photo. You could see it in the warmth of their smiles and the twinkles in their big, bright eyes. I say this because when I look back at old photos of my son, he has the same unabashed look of pure joy spreading across his face that says, "Oh boy, someone I love is paying attention to me." I couldn't help but contrast this with photos I'd seen in other cases of kids from backgrounds filled with abuse, fear, and pain, where typically there was no smile at all or only a forced-looking one.

Even now, nearly thirty years later, I remember with surprising clarity the weekend I first read through the *Doe* case record and came face to face with the horrific facts. I can even remember that, as I read through it with the fire crackling behind me, I was constantly contrasting the calm normality of my own childhood, and that of my son's, with the tumultuous, wild ride that life had given the Doe children. I can easily picture myself that first evening of reading the Doe case record, when I told my son yet another installment of the bedtime story he so loved, *The Elephant Trainer Boy*. The story was a tale I made up, chapter by chapter, relating the adventures of an Indian boy whose father trained elephants that the boy delivered across all of India, despite his youth. It was easy for the boy, you see, because unbeknownst to everybody, even his father, he had learned Pachydermese. Why was this night different from all other nights? Why was just another normal, loving bedtime with my son so etched into my mind? It took me years to understand that it was the sharpness of the contrast between his life and that of the Doe children.

No sooner was my boy asleep than I dove back into the Doe files. Remarkably, the disclosure of the rampant and abusive sexuality inside the family household had come to light only by accident. The children's mother, who was on public relief and had counseling available to her, voluntarily sought guidance about why she felt so insecure when applying for jobs. Ashley had tagged along with her mother, and in the corner of the waiting room she spotted a satchel that had a doll's hand protruding from it. But what she found when she opened the little bag were not just ordinary dolls. These were what social workers call anatomically correct dolls, which are used by mental health professionals as an aid in determining if very young children have seen or experienced sexualized interactions. When the social worker found Ashley playing all-too knowledgeably with the dolls, she immediately filed a report with the DSS.

The department investigated the household that very evening, which culminated in an emergency removal of the two children and their placement in separate, temporary foster homes. During the weeks that followed, the children were interviewed by a Sexual Assault Intervention Network team, specialized clinical social workers, DSS personnel, the police, and the prosecutorial authorities handling the criminal cases against the perpetrators. The department brought an emergency court proceeding to take legal custody of the children, which was allowed. That was the end of the family: the children would never see any of the adults again.

The police arrested the children's grandparents, their mother, their aunt, and their uncle. Within a matter of weeks, a plea bargain was negotiated with the mother, who was considered by the police to be as much a victim as a perpetrator. She was allowed to avoid criminal prosecution in exchange for permanently releasing legal custody of the two children to the commonwealth. I later learned that she also agreed to immediately move out of Massachusetts forever and to never again seek to have contact with her children. To the best of my knowledge, she was never heard from again. While there was arguably some justice to this outcome given her limited capacities and her own victimization, I could find no justice whatsoever in the disposition of the criminal charges against the grandmother and step-grandfather. Incredibly, they were allowed to plead guilty to several felony counts, and in exchange for their written covenant never to return and never to attempt to make contact with the children, they also were allowed to leave the state. As chance would have it, in the years that followed, I came to know the judge who had ruled on the matter, and I only barely refrained from bringing up the case and excoriating His Honor for such a blatant miscarriage of justice. The disposition of the criminal charges against the aunt and the uncle was never known to me, although I did come to understand that they too were barred from ever having contact with the children again.

In the normal course of things, the children were moved from their two temporary shelter foster homes to two different, long-term foster homes. Not surprisingly, they each languished. Seth's record indicated that from the day of his removal from his birth family, his affect became almost entirely flat. To quote his foster mother, "Seth has never smiled—not once."

Ashley's record showed that she seldom played or interacted in any way with the other children in her foster home. She reportedly spent most of her time "staring off into space." The record also indicated, sadly, that while visitation between the children was clinically indicated and favored by all, because of the overly heavy caseloads of their DSS social workers, only two brief visits between the children actually occurred in the fourteen months prior to their preadoptive placement with the plaintiffs. So during this difficult period in their lives, the children had not only lost the adults in their family—forever—but had also lost each other. They were both alone, terribly alone, for these critically important transition months.

Notwithstanding the circumstances described above, both children were still consistently described in the record as "intelligent" and "articulate" by the myriad of adult professionals with whom they now dealt. Each child openly and honestly answered questions put to them by mental health professionals and other adults, and they were able to describe their lives in their birth home with remarkable clarity. What particularly caught my eye, however, was that in each and every investigative report I read, whether written by the police, the district attorney, DSS social workers, or the psychologists who provided clinical counseling to the children after their removal from the birth home, the children were quoted as expressing *love and concern* for their birth family, including their grandparents. Understandably, even admirably, they also repeatedly expressed a great deal of worried concern about what would become of their hapless mother.

*

More than a year passed in long-term foster care, and the children, now eleven and nine, were rapidly deteriorating. Seth was beginning to show significant signs of clinical depression, and Ashley was increasingly despondent and removed. Both children appeared joyless and limpid; the notes of their respective clinicians indicated that the only spark of life either child exhibited in clinical sessions was when they fantasized about being reunited in an adoptive home. Fortunately for them, that was exactly what the DSS had in mind.

Susan Sears's agency specialized in the adoptive placement of older sibling groups, which was why DSS referred the Doe children to her. She almost immediately thought of a couple that her agency had precleared to adopt a sibling group and gave them a call to ascertain their interest. From Sears's point of view, this couple seemed ideal: they were a two-income, upper-middle-class family whose large home could easily provide a separate bedroom for each child. And just as importantly in Sears's eyes, both the wife and husband had successfully completed graduate work. Sears felt that their advanced level of education would prove useful, given the massive amount of sensitive information they would need to read and absorb about the children's background prior to making their decision as to whether these were the right children for them to adopt.

And indeed, we know from the deposition testimony of the parents that Sears was correct: the couple actually did read the same written record I had pored through. They both later testified that they were stunned by what the siblings had endured—anyone would be. So stunned, apparently, that they felt very unsure about proceeding with the adoption. But in the midst of all their quite reasonable uncertainty, something short-circuited the careful deliberation and due diligence the parents had initially planned to undertake in thinking through the complexities of this potential sibling adoption. These were educated, thoughtful people who would by nature be cautious. I was convinced that there would be no way to directly probe the parents to find out what had interfered with the process that had been planned, since there was a high probability they themselves would not have been aware of exactly what had happened. All that we later learned was that the prospective adoptive parents stopped all serious balancing of the pros and cons the day they met the children. My own guess is that this was a product of how monumentally good-looking these two siblings were. On top of this, I don't find it at all hard to understand how the potential adoptive parents got caught up in the children's exuberance at being reunited. And thus the die was cast.

The lawsuit, of course, displaced the parents' aborted due diligence process onto my client. But in this effort, the parents' suit had a problem because the file held a copy of just the kind of letter that trial attorneys dream of finding: Sears had written to the potential adoptive parents advising the couple to retain the services of their own consulting psychologist to advise them about the complexities of adopting survivors of childhood sexual abuse. And in fact, the couple had done so. Better yet (for us), the record contained a copy of the report submitted to them by their consulting psychologist. It clearly stated that children from such a background can act out in severe and unpredictable ways—unpredictable being the operative word. They were told about the behavioral patterns that are the most prevalent in children who were sexually abused at a young age, the most typical one for girls being teenage promiscuity and for boys being sexual predation. They were, in sum, sternly warned by their own consulting psychologist.

The adoption fantasy—for both parents and the children—clearly snowballed the day of the children's first visit to the home of the potential adoptive couple. Ashley told us far later in the litigation that the day of the first visit "was like Dorothy getting taken by the hurricane [sic] to the land of Oz." I remember smiling when she testified using this term, but I knew exactly what she meant. Adoption in Massachusetts often means upward social mobility for a child, since it is frequently young women of modest means who choose to place a child for adoption, while it is mostly couples of significant means who experience infertility due to waiting longer to start their family. But this case was extreme. The children had grown up in a simple, prefabricated wooden rental house in a proper but humble neighborhood. In stark contrast, the Does' home was a striking central entrance colonial that sat just at the top of a sizable hill in a tony neighborhood town just outside of Boston. Running downhill from the house was a massive yard, which the children each described as a park. It was nearly an acre in size—a virtual sea of perfectly manicured lawn. Better still, the property backed up to a vast nature preserve, and there was talk that day of all manner of enticing ideas, including a discussion about the possibility of constructing a tree house in the massive oak that grew at one end of the lawn just before the woods began. What seemed crystal clear from all we learned was that during that first visit, the children fell in love with the concept of being reunited and living in a fairy-tale house on the top of a hill, while the parents fell in love with the concept of having two such stunningly beautiful children.

The placement went very well indeed. Ashley and Seth were remarkably intact and were thrilled to escape the depressing loneliness they had each endured in their foster homes. These bright children understood that they now had a chance for a very different type of life. Here were parents who knew how to prepare one to face the world, and something in these two children drove them to take advantage of this. The children excelled in every way in the local school, and, according to the parents' testimony, were a delight to have in the adoptive home. The one hiccup was that, at the end of the mandatory six-month trial period before the adoption could be legally finalized, Seth, who had just turned thirteen, asked the Does if he could postpone these legal formalities. He reported to his clinical social worker that, although he liked living with his new family, he remained anxious about the fate of his mother. He just felt he couldn't permanently cut his connection to her—not yet. Ashley, on the other hand, wanted legal finalization to happen as soon as possible, and she was enthusiastically in favor of proceeding. To the credit of the adoptive couple, they had no qualms about the older child's reluctance to finalize his adoption at that point and took no offense from his admirable loyalty to his vanished mother. Sears's notes in the record were clear on this point: the couple felt that sometimes only the passage of time can heal great wounds, and they were determined to be patient out of respect for Seth's needs. In the meantime, they finalized the adoption of Ashley, and the Doe story seemed to be on its way to a happy ending.

*

Ah, but a different fate awaited them. Late one night, about eighteen months after the placement, the parents discovered that their adopted daughter and her brother had a full and completely secret sex life. The couple was shocked and horrified, understandably. They were furious with Seth, again, understandably. But then Mrs. Doe lost it, screaming at Seth and calling him a rapist. But that was nothing compared with the precipitous action she took next—a decision that would have devastating consequences for everyone in the family: the police were summoned.

Barely an hour after the children had been discovered together, Seth was led away in handcuffs, with Ashley watching. By noon, the boy was irretrievably caught up in the machinery of the Massachusetts Juvenile Justice System, which would change his life forever. By late that afternoon, the parents had cut all ties with the mental health professionals who had been counseling Ashley throughout the adoption proceedings and replaced them with a new clinician who specialized in therapy for rape victims. Ashley was now branded and stigmatized—and bereft of the brother she so loved.

*

Once Attorney O'Toole returned my call, I was able to begin learning how he planned to present the case. From his point of view, the gravamen (that is, the grievance) of the lawsuit was simple and straightforward: the department, the mental health professionals, and most assuredly my adoption agency clients, had all been grossly negligent in failing to give the parents adequate warning that the children might act out sexually with one another. Moreover, O'Toole concluded, this negligence led directly to a state of total chaos in the adoptive household, causing great and irreparable injuries to the parents and to Ashley. I remember well the summary line he added: "My case is simple. Elegantly so."

I also remember that I failed to find a way to contest this for quite some time. The case certainly had a unique and compelling fact pattern, with children who had first lost their birth home and then experienced still more loss with the adoption disruption.

Before I could find words to respond, O'Toole ominously quoted an old hymn: "Snow, on snow, on snow. That's what we have here: loss, on loss, on loss."

He was right. He had a case with significant damages and a powerful argument. If the plaintiffs' claim of professional negligence could be sold to a jury, there was definitely the potential here for punitive damages. And if a jury is out to make a point—to punish, to teach a lesson—they could mete out punitive damages in very large amounts. This was not at all what Rhonda Wilkins was hiring me to produce as an outcome, nor what Susan Sears could live with as a blight on her professional reputation. But I remained flummoxed.

I asked a number of questions, principally to gain time to think. O'Toole droned on, but I was no longer listening. I was racking my brain during his righteous monologue to find some argument—any argument—against his position. I had been taught as a fledgling defense attorney that it was critically important to put doubt in a plaintiff's attorney's mind from the very outset of a case. But I still didn't see a counterargument, as I focused in again on O'Toole's words. He was in the midst of boasting about how strong his liability case was because he had already located and retained an expert who would testify that my clients should have better trained and equipped the adoptive parents for the challenge they were taking on. Basically, although he refrained from saying it directly, he was arguing that Sears should have forewarned the parents that the children might act out sexually with each other.

Having thought of nothing clever, and being out of time, I played the only card I had in my hand: my previous career. "Jeff, you don't know my background, but the only reason the insurer gave me this case to defend is because I have a PhD in the field. I used to teach courses on children and trauma at Boston University. And I couldn't disagree more with your expert's view. If only we *did* know enough to foresee and predict human behavior with such clarity." O'Toole was silent; he had no doctorate to throw up against mine. "But we don't. We have no way of being able to predict whether and how children rescued from abusive backgrounds will act. There are a thousand different possible behavioral reactions, and your clients were told about the most common patterns."

Having retaken the initiative, I wasn't about to give it up. When he started to speak, I plowed right on, adlibbing as I went. "Don't you see? The jury is going to hate the knee-jerk reaction of your clients to the children's sexual acting out. As I understand it, they didn't even wait until the morning to garner the advice of their own consulting psychologist or any other mental health professional. How are you going to get around that?"

O'Toole stammered a bit, and then asked me what alternative reaction they could possibly have had—and it was in replying to this question that I found the argument that would later prove critical to the resolution of the case.

"If I had been consulted by your clients after their discovery, I would have told them that the *last* people they wanted to call were the police. I would have advised them to handle the sexuality as a family matter, exhibiting connection and commitment to both children. Personally, I would have counseled that, as strange as it may seem, in the very discovery of the intersibling sexuality, the adoptive parents had stumbled on an enormous opportunity to make these children their own. They could have initiated discussions about sexual boundaries the children had never been taught, and in doing so, they could have become the very parents the children needed. Everybody could have won, Jeff, instead of everybody losing."

It was working. O'Toole remained silent, so I took the opportunity to ask him how he felt about Ashley losing her brother—the last family member in her life—*all because his clients didn't take the time to consult professionals about how to react to what they had learned.* To O'Toole's credit, he regained his voice and replied, if in a considerably less assertive tone.

"Look, Terry, I feel terrible about Ashley's additional loss, of course, but I'm her attorney, not her social worker."

"Well, the jury is going to feel terrible about it too, and if I do my job decently, they're going to blame your clients for their precipitous reaction that cost Ashley her brother. They're going to hear my expert testify that, with patience and professional input, they could have developed an understanding as to why these children were so sexualized and come up with a strategy about how to proceed. And they're going to hear that with those insights and that strategy, they could have built a successful adoptive family. That's what I'm going to argue to the jury, Jeff, and I promise you, I'll find just the right forensic psychiatrist to support that argument."

O'Toole was silent now, the way a bull goes still when the matador puzzles him into tighter and tighter circles with good cape work. Damn, I enjoyed the chess-like games of trial work. Game on.

*

This initial telephone conference was the first step in what turned out to be the better part of three years of litigation in the case. Because the plaintiffs had sued so many parties, every legal step in the lawsuit involved thirteen law offices—a logistical nightmare from a scheduling point of view. During this period, every imaginable person having anything to do with the children was deposed under oath. The records produced by so many witnesses were prodigious: over ten thousand separate documents were formally numbered and entered into the record. The most important deponents were, of course, the children, followed by the adoptive parents. The depositions of these four principal parties to the action lasted for three full days—each. Susan Sears and her two agency employees were examined for two days each, and there were day-long depositions of every single clinician who had ever worked with the children after their removal from the birth home. But it didn't end there: additional full-day depositions were taken from all the children's teachers and guidance counselors, the four sets of foster parents who had kept Ashley and Seth before their placement with the adoptive parents, every member of the clinical and milieu staff who had worked with Seth in his sexual offender program, and all of the children's treating doctors.

As the months passed, I began to develop the theory of the case that had come to me in that first telephone call with Attorney O'Toole. More and more I came to believe that the best defense of the case would be to take the offensive. It was critical to blame the adoptive parents for so quickly jettisoning

Seth and thereby branding Ashley. It was they who had placed stigmatizing labels on these lost children: one as a rapist, the other as a rape victim. It hadn't had to be that way.

Above and beyond that, the adoptive parents could also be faulted for causing Ashley to suffer through the agony of a lawsuit. These people didn't need the money; it would be easy to demonstrate that to the jury. The lawsuit as brought by the adoptive parents required Ashley to give detailed testimony in response to the probing questions of *eleven* opposing attorneys. Even more invasive, arguably, was the right the judge granted the defense to have Ashley examined by the defense's own expert psychiatrist. And this examination would not be designed to be clinically therapeutic: its goal would be to probe the psychological health of Ashley in order to try to ascertain how the adoption disruption had injured her—above and beyond how she had been injured by the incest in and the loss of her birth family.

Everything that was true for Ashley was true for Seth as well. As the boy had neither biological nor adoptive parents, the court had appointed a guardian ad litem to protect his interests in the matter, and the guardian had hired separate counsel to add Seth into the lawsuit as an additional plaintiff. So Seth was deposed and examined by the psychiatric expert witness just as Ashley was, and the jury would need to work through whether they saw him as a perpetrator or as another victim—or both.

Once I had settled on my working theory of the case— that the culprits in these children's lives were the adults, not each other—I could begin thinking through an appropriate trial strategy. It may seem counterintuitive, but trial planning begins at the end and works back. The very first things to identify are the principal themes of the closing argument you want to make to the jury. From there, the trial attorney works backward to discover the evidence and arrange for the expert opinion that would be needed to support the argument. Of course, one has to keep one's mind open to react appropriately to what is learned in the discovery process, but that being said, at any given time, an experienced trial attorney knows exactly what his argument to the jury would be if the trial were to begin the following morning. I once had a case where this principle saved the day: all counsel had appeared at a routine pretrial hearing to have the court rule on some pretrial motions, and the judge, who had just had a case settle that opened up a full week-long gap in her trial schedule, precipitously scheduled trial to begin at nine o'clock the following morning.

Anyway, in the *Doe* case, it was clear that success would turn on finding just the right forensic psychiatrist to argue that the parents' reaction to their revelation did as much or more harm to Ashley as whatever harm came from the intersibling sexuality. And something else that had been drilled into my head in my early trial law training: you have got to have the "alpha" expert in the case. In other words, your expert needs to trump the opposing side's expert—above and beyond the substance of whatever they may argue about your case. This is because many jurors, when overwhelmed by incompatible expert testimony, end up comparing the experts themselves rather than the conflicting explanatory models they present. Accordingly, you want your expert to have gone to Harvard not Podunk, to have worked on important real-world projects to which the jurors can relate, and to have arguably national or international renown, not merely local reputation. And you also want an expert who has a winning forensic presence— either because he or she is charismatic or good-looking—or because their presence *as a person* is alluring for some other reason.

Richard Putnam, MD, fit the bill. He was a board-certified psychiatrist connected to Harvard Medical School who had largely been responsible for founding the field of trauma psychiatry and who regularly lectured throughout the United States and, for that matter, around the world. And on top of all that, he was strikingly handsome, with a commanding presence in a courtroom derived in significant part from his bass-baritone voice: it filled a courtroom. There were only two problems with Putnam: first, he was famously reluctant to take on new forensic work, and second, he was enormously expensive.

It was time to bite the bullet and call Rhonda Wilkins, the insurance claim agent on the case, and therefore my boss. She would, after all, be the person in charge of approving Dr. Putnam's staggering bills. She answered in her patented New Jersey accent after only one ring, and once I talked her through my current theory of the case, her immediate reaction—interrupting me toward the end of my little presentation—was, and I quote (imagine the accent yourself), "That scares the fuck out of me. It's an all or nothing gamble. Either you bring a juror all the way over to blaming the adoptive parents for freaking out, or you royally piss them off by insulting the couple who opened their home to these wild kids and then got fucked for trying to help. And you wouldn't have a chance of arguing this unless you can find the right shrink to back you up. And even if you did, the approach could still blow up in your face at trial. Something about it I don't like." She went silent—a rare thing for Wilkins as she thought further. "Why do I think you already have someone in mind?"

"Ah, good question," I responded. "Remember Dr. Putnam? We used him two years ago in that suicide case?"

"Grab him," she interrupted. "I sure the fuck don't want him showing up on the other side. But do us both a favor here: be very, very sure Putnam's testimony will support your theory before you adopt that idea with finality. We'll be royally fucked if you try what you're talking about and the jury likes the parents more than they like Putnam." With that, she hung up—no good-bye, no anything.

I was armed with Dr. Putnam's home number from the previous case we had worked on together, but it still took me over a week to hear back from him. Almost the first words out of his mouth were about how extraordinarily busy he was and how he was only taking on forensic cases that were interesting to him from a research perspective. He asked point blank, "Be honest with me. Is there any research potential here? I'm asking Terry the PhD, not Terry the lawyer. Anything interesting here?"

"Rick," I shot back, trying to sound as confident as possible, "I have a theory of this case that you may or may not be able to support once you've examined the children. But if I've got it right, there is extremely significant research potential here."

I proceeded to relay the details of the boundaryless sexuality in the three-generational birth family, along with the highly unusual—maybe unique—fact that it took place in a framework of what otherwise seemed to be perfectly normal parental love and nurturing. And I filled him in on what had happened with the children since.

"Have you met the children?" Putnam asked.

"No," I responded. "But those who have report that they were remarkably intact at the time of their removal from the birth home. My own guess at this point—and of course, what will count will be your examination findings—is that these children were psychologically unscathed by the sexuality in their birth home because of the environment in which it took place. I have a feeling that the first truly traumatic event to occur to them was probably the loss and criminalization of their birth family. The children never saw them again after the evening of the discovery when the department removed the children on an emergency basis. And they'll never see any of them again, ever. It was part of all the plea bargains. One moment they had this big crazy family, and the next thing they knew, the family was gone forever."

I could tell it was working. "That's an amazing proposition," Putnam said in his basso profundo voice after a significant pause to think through what I had said. "You're right though. It would be a unique set of facts, if you've got it right. I've never heard of that pattern." There was another long pause. "I'll take the case, but only if I am allowed to perform a serious psychiatric examination of both children. I won't do it without that. And before that I'll need to read the entire written record of everything that's known about the kids, about their birth family, and about the circumstances in the adoptive family. And for the examination I'll need no fewer than three two-hour sessions with each of the children. If you can get me all that, I'll write a report and testify for you. But, will the insurer pay for me to do all that? It's going to take me a ton of time."

I assured Putnam that I already had insurance company preapproval and also a plan to arrange for his bills to be shared by the ten different insurance companies in the case for the multiple defendants.

There was no problem with the latter idea. Within a week, I had the agreement of each of the other defendants' attorneys to share the cost of the expert witness, since his testimony was in the interest of our entire side of the case. Within another week, I had a full copy of the records messengered over to Putnam's office.

The only problem arose elsewhere. Attorney O'Toole adamantly refused the examination request, taking the position that Dr. Putnam could learn what he needed to know from reading Ashley's existing psychiatric chart and speaking with her current treating clinicians. Adding another psychiatrist to the mix, he argued, could upset Ashley, who was fragile.

So ten days later, off to court went all dozen attorneys to put the matter before the trial judge. Every once in a while in court you can feel the judge hurrying along your argument because he or she already has the gist of what you're saying, and wants to take the matter up him- or herself with the other side. The trick as an attorney in these situations is to quickly conclude and get out of the line of fire. And sure enough, as it turned out, the judge had her own very strong reaction to Attorney O'Toole's argument.

"Then don't bring the lawsuit if you think it might harm the child," she told him. "Your clients are the ones who made the decision to put the girl through this. So here are your two options, Counselor: drop the suit, or submit her to the examination. Make a decision. Now."

It was either check or checkmate, and O'Toole chose the former. He replied forcefully that he was not withdrawing the lawsuit and agreed to work out an examination schedule with me. He also shot me an icy stare that spoke volumes about the likely degree of cooperation I would get in the case from that point on.

Roughly two months later, which was still well before when the first of Putnam's psychiatric examinations was scheduled, I received a twenty-four-page report from him summing up his reaction to the massive written record of the children's background. I was thrilled with the quality of work the report evidenced and immediately called Putnam's secretary to make an appointment.

Two weeks later, on a sunny and unusually warm day in late spring almost a year after I had first received the *Doe* case, I met with Putnam. In his private practice, he worked out of the basement of the century-old Boston brownstone in which he and his family lived. The office was a warm, friendly room with a working fireplace, and gently worn burgundy-colored leather chairs. Two of the walls were covered with floor-to-ceiling bookcases, and in one of them I could see the three main books Putnam had authored on trauma issues; each of these books was shelved next to its translations in five or six different foreign languages. I was still salivating at the thought of how easy it was going to be to sell Putnam's expertise to the jury when he entered, unseen, from a side room. Without pleasantries, he jumped right into the heart of the matter.

"Two things, Terry. First, how in the hell is the plaintiffs' attorney planning to argue damages from the adoption disruption, given what these children went through in their birth home? I don't even understand how he can do that. And second, and here's the good news for you, I don't think your clients were negligent or unprofessional. There is no way in hell they could have predicted this sexual acting out, I can assure you. But tell me how you think plaintiffs' counsel intends to argue his damages case. I just don't get what the logic of it can be, do you?"

"Actually, I do know what he has in mind," I responded. "He's going to tell the jury that the breakup of the adoptive home caused *new damages* to these vulnerable children. He said he's going to argue that there was additional harm through aggravation of the original harm. Tough argument to make, but not impossible."

"I still don't see how he's going to pull that off," Putnam shot back. "Especially because I buy your theory that to the extent the kids were harmed by the adoption disruption, the origin of any 'additional harm' more likely came from the heartless handling of the discovery of the sexuality. And by the way, I was horrified to read that Seth was adjudicated a sexual offender. That is a gross miscarriage of justice—at least from what I know at this point. And the other side of the coin, obviously, is that Ashley was certainly *not* a rape victim. Hell, she was as clear as she could be with the police that she co-initiated and willfully participated on an equal basis. And from what I read, I think there's every reason to believe her. So here's your takeaway: subject to what I learn in my examinations of the children, at this point I can give you some very strong testimony to back up your argument." Putnam paused after delivering this good news, thinking about something. "You know what I really want to learn about in the examinations?" he asked. "I want to dig into what feelings, what *emotions* the sexual behavior generated for each of the kids. I want to know what it *meant* to the two of them. I really think this may give us the key to understand what was really going on."

"And what about Seth?"

"Yeah, I've been thinking about him. I definitely want to learn what he experienced in the sexual offender program. I'd love to know whether or not the program personnel felt that he was an offender. I mean, above and beyond the fact that they were being paid to treat him as one."

"Actually, I know," I kicked in. "I was general counsel to that program for a decade, and I'm good pals with its clinical director. I ran into her at a seminar a few months ago and spoke with her about the kid—way off the record. And it's just what you would expect. She told me straight up that she doesn't think Seth is a good fit for their program. That's how she put it. She just doesn't see him as an offender acting out a compulsion disorder. But Rick, the kid is stuck in a crazy catch-twenty-two. The program is pure behavior modification. There are no exceptions, apparently, so Seth would need to admit a sexual aggression problem before the program's protocol would allow him to advance at all. He'll be on level one *forever* unless he lies about it. Sad stuff, no?"

Putnam shook his head. "Poor kid. He'll be branded for life, whatever the clinical director says off the record."

We spent an additional hour and a half going over documents in the record to prepare Putnam for his upcoming examinations of the children. It was obvious how focused and excited Putnam was about the exams. It was also pretty clear to me that what he learned from this one-off case would almost certainly be reported at some upcoming psychiatric meeting.

Needless to say, it was fabulous to learn that Putnam came out the same way I did about the impact of the adoptive parents' reaction to their discovery of the intersibling sexuality. This meant I could reassure Wilkins of the theory of the case I was promoting, and it was time to do so. She was easy to reach, as always; somehow I had the distinct impression the woman basically lived at her desk. "Rhonda, Terry Freiberg about the *Doe* case," I began.

"I know which fucking case you're on, Terry. I call it my 'nightmare case.' We've reserved two million for it. Two fucking million dollars. That's the policy limit. And this is completely dumping my department's numbers in the toilet. I'm holding you personally responsible for the looks my supervisor gives me in the hallway, and he was an unpleasant son of a bitch even before this damn case came along."

"Rhonda," I wedged in, "I've got good news. Putnam is on board with the theory that the biggest stressor the kids ever faced beyond what went on in their birth home was how the adoptive parents handled the intersibling sexuality. He'll give us just the testimony I need to pull this off."

She was silent for a moment, disappointed at being drawn into conversation and away from excoriating me.

"It still frightens me," she replied, in a quiet voice she must have borrowed from someone down the hall. "So do us both a favor: keep your mind open to finding an alternative approach. See if you can't create an option that isn't so high risk."

"Fair enough. Open minds are good things."

"Okay. Go for it." Dial tone. Goddamn it. Why couldn't the woman say good-bye or ciao or something? Everyone else does.

*

By this time in the case, each of the defendant agencies and individual mental health professionals had produced every document in their respective files on the children. While some of the documents appeared in more than one professional's file, and hence were redundant, the total number of stamped documents was just over ten thousand pages. That's a lot of trees. At this point, it was time to schedule depositions. On the defense side, we identified just over seventy people we wanted to depose, and of course, the plaintiffs would have their own list of deponents.

Soon after this, the seemingly endless series of Tuesday depositions began. It ended up taking more than eighteen months' worth of Tuesdays. I thought about shifting the responsibility for some of the depositions to an associate attorney who had been helping me with the written record, but Wilkins would not hear of it. As she phrased it, "I want you to know every one of these fucking witnesses personally. You take your own personal ass into that conference room, and don't give me some fucking associate who'll leave your firm before this case goes to trial. Understand?"

I remember answering her command with a sarcastic "Yes, sir," but it was to no avail—she never heard the "sir" part.

While the depositions were tedious and often duplicative from a legal point of view, they were absolutely fascinating from a social psychological research perspective. Let's face it, social scientists have trouble gathering good data; they are usually dependent on the acuity of perception and the accuracy of reporting of those they interview. And they can't interview everyone they want to; people don't have to submit to that. But lawyers have the force of the law to subpoena anyone they want to examine—and to question witnesses under oath after warning them that they are testifying subject to "the pains and penalties of perjury." What a sweet little research tool!

The depositions were designed to uncover everything that any adult who had known the children had ever observed or learned about them. We deposed each of the four sets of foster parents, every teacher or school counselor who had encountered one or both of the children, and every medical doctor, social worker, psychologist, and psychiatrist who had treated either child along the way. During this process, we learned the most minute of details about every aspect of the children's lives, beginning the first moment after their removal from the birth home. And, of course, we immersed ourselves in an equally detailed examination of what occurred to the children after the adoption disruption. We also spoke to four witnesses who described Seth's progressive deterioration after his delinquency adjudication and subsequent placement in the commonwealth's Department of Youth Services. We deposed every mental health and teaching professional who had worked clinically or educationally with either child. The witnesses varied between those who had no memories of the children, and who could therefore only interpret their written notes for us, and those whose memories of the children were vivid and fresh.

I will never forget the tearful sobbing of one young clinical social worker who testified that she had seen Ashley up to about six months before the date of her deposition. With tears running down her cheeks, she described to us what it was like to listen to Ashley struggle to define herself as a rape victim. This clinician was remarkably open with us. In her opinion, Ashley was using the term *rape victim* because she had been coached that it would benefit the cause of her lawsuit. I looked over at Attorney O'Toole when this little gem came out. Lo and behold, he was looking down at his notepad, furiously pretending to scribble away. The social worker concluded with another small bomb: when she had asked the adoptive parents to come in to discuss this ingenuous self-labeling, she had been summarily dismissed.

Among the more interesting depositions were those of the four sets of very experienced foster parents who had known the children, particularly the two couples who had observed the children the night they were taken from their birth family. All eight of these witnesses reported the same reaction to the two kids: they were horrifically sad at being ripped out of their home, and they showed no signs of relief at finding a safe environment, as abused children typically do. The foster parents also reported that they found the children remarkably intact and well behaved. And all eight of these highly experienced observers reported consistently with one another on another matter of central importance to my theory of the case. The four who had known Ashley reported that they had never seen her show the first sign of exhibiting what clinicians call sexually reactive behavior (that is, overly sexualized and/or abnormally sexually available). Likewise, the four who knew Seth confirmed that he had never acted in a sexually aggressive manner toward another foster child. The evidentiary quality of these observations was magnified nicely by the fact that I had two completely independent sets of highly experienced witnesses who corroborated one another on each child. And, of course, Putnam could testify that being sexually reactive or sexually aggressive cannot be turned on and off at will. We both felt strongly that these observations by the foster parents corroborated our suspicion that the intersibling sexuality that took place in the adoptive home was something other than garden-variety sexual contact. The key to the case, we were more certain than ever, lay in discerning just what the children's sexuality was all about *to them.* Could intercourse be about something other than sex?

There was, of course, one terribly important era from the children's past that was impossible to learn much about. What precisely had they experienced in their birth home? Of course, we read and reread the reports the children had given to the

Sexual Assault Intervention Network and to the police right after their removal from the home. But these are about what happened, not what the home was like. And these were just the children's views of what went on. Additionally, search as I might, I never located a photo of the inside of the residence. There were no social services used by the family (remember, the kids were thriving at school), so no DSS files. And, of course, the adults in the family were all gone with the wind to parts unknown. I have to admit that part of my beef with the trial judge who let them off was that if he'd put the grandfather and grandmother in prison, where they belonged, in my opinion, I would have known where to find them to take their depositions. But now, no such luck. So as for learning what went on in the family home, Putnam in his examinations and I in my depositions would have to get the story from the children, and they would be our only source of information. We wanted to learn how they were nurtured, fed, medically cared for, bathed, clothed, supervised as they did homework, ferried to hobbies and sports, and so on. The problem, of course, was that children seldom notice the details of all of this parental work. All children are basically oblivious to the scores of things adults do to raise them and make a household work.

With the depositions and examinations of the children soon to come, Putnam and I decided to meet to think through the approach each of us would use in our respective spheres. As soon as his schedule allowed, we met one evening after work at his office and walked to a small French bistro he favored in Boston's South End. Entering into the stillness of the restaurant with its checkered tablecloths was a delight in and of itself—there were cool spring winds gusting about outside, and the walk over had been brisker than my suit jacket could handle. Putnam ordered up a bottle of Argentinian Malbec and a cheese platter, and asked the waiter's indulgence while we spoke together before ordering.

Putnam had come to work. Even before the wine arrived, he announced that we were going to reason out *tonight* a theory about what we thought the intersibling sexuality meant to the two children. This theory would need to account for the fact that the sexuality occurred *despite* the fact that there was ample evidence that Seth was not sexually aggressive and Ashley was not sexually reactive. In addition, our hypothesis would need to account for a new fact that had just come to light: both children had been prepubescent at the time of their sexual encounters in the adoptive home. We knew this new fact with confidence because my private eye had finally located a clinical professional who had moved out of state and been nearly impossible to locate. This clinical social worker was in the habit of videotaping his sessions with children, and he had filmed Seth during the era when he lived in the adoptive home. When you looked at the tape, it was crystal clear that you were looking at a boy who had not yet been through puberty. So what was taking place? Why would prepubescent, nonsexually aggressive children be having sex?

Putnam leaned back in his chair and swirled the dark-red Malbec around and around in his glass, staring intently at it. After a goodly pause, he asked me to think about what touching—hugging and being hugged—means to small children. Then, before I could answer, he turned toward me and seemingly on a whim asked me how many hugs and kisses I'd lavished on my son in his first five years. I remember my response word for word: "Got to be a million. Definitely a million."

"Exactly," he responded with emphasis. "Exactly. Now imagine if you and your wife just stopped one day, if suddenly there were no more kisses, no more hugs. Think how absent all that touch and warmth would be to your child, how he would *hunger* for it. Now think of what the Doe children experienced. In their birth home, they had the million kisses—but it didn't end there: the touching knew no limits.

Put aside for the moment that from an outside perspective they were being sexually abused. Just for a moment, think of what they experienced as hyperintensified touching. Now think of this: these children went from this hypertouching to absolutely zero touching. From the moment they were removed from their home, there was no more touching *at all* in their lives. The foster homes they went to were completely touch-free environments—because touching was strictly forbidden by DSS regulations. Can you imagine how the Doe kids must have been *starved* for physical soothing by the time they were placed together eighteen months later in the adoptive home? And while I need to confirm this with the kids in their examinations, let's assume the adoptive parents rarely touched these kids who they barely knew." Putnam paused to finally taste his well-swirled Malbec. "Who knows?" he mused. "Perhaps to these children the intersibling sexuality was just their substitute for the normal touching most children their age get on a daily basis from their parents. I wouldn't be surprised if the Doe kids didn't even conceive of what they were doing as sex. They may have just experienced it as mutual soothing and nothing more."

Putnam leaned forward in his chair to cut a slice of cheese. What he said made perfect sense. Whatever these children were experiencing, it was likely to be very different from how it looked to adults outside their circle who would immediately classify it as incestuous sex. We clearly had our work cut out for us in the upcoming depositions and examinations.

After we had eaten, Putnam and I agreed that a glass of port sounded like a good idea—especially when compared to heading out into the windy chill. Our conversation turned to what we needed to learn about the adoptive parents in their upcoming depositions. I described how I had designed questions intended to probe their upbringing, their education, their early careers in the Catholic Church, their decision to leave the Church, their secular careers, the origin of their decision to adopt a sibling group of older children, the adoption training they had (or didn't have), and of course, any and all details about what they had been told about how the children might behave. I also intended to fully probe what they had heard from their own consulting psychologist about the difficulties and risks involved in adopting older children from a sexually abusive background, and why and by what logic they had determined to override his warnings.

Putnam went on to list a number of areas of inquiry that really mattered to him, including one issue in particular that he emphasized as critical. Leaning forward and looking me straight in the eyes, he pleaded with me. "I need to know—I absolutely need to know—what exactly the Does were thinking that night when they called the police. Something's up here, something we don't know yet. It doesn't add up. And you may have to push. It's deep down, but it's there. Just promise me you'll try. I want to learn as much as I can from your deposition transcripts before I design my examinations."

I did promise, and after we shook hands outside the restaurant and I was heading up the street to the T stop, I kept thinking about how I should approach this issue. The only strategy I came up with was to be doggedly persistent. I would keep approaching the issue from different angles, hoping that one of my questions would somehow unlock the door to Putnam's mysterious "something."

And so the day arrived when it was time to depose John and Jane Doe. If I had to describe them in three words, they would be prim and proper. The two parents were entirely formal in dress and manner: upper-middle-class individuals who seemed to take their social status very seriously. Each was lean, with nary an extra pound. They both responded to questions in a terse, almost military manner. There were no wasted words, essentially zero body language, no moments of warmth, and never a single smile from either of them. Usually, I later told Putnam, in tense circumstances like a deposition or even at trial, witnesses search for at least one opportunity to smile. This often happens at a break in the drama, when the judge is called off the bench by a telephone call from his wife or some such. I had always thought witnesses did it to take a momentary break from the tension, but as the years went by, I began to think it had more to do with a witness just wanting to exhibit that there were pleasant facets to his or her personality not being displayed on the stand. In any case, there was not one single smile from either of the Does, not in six days of deposition. This, and everything else about them, gave me the distinct impression that what really mattered most to them was being in control.

Given that my tactic was to approach the topic of sexuality as indirectly as possible, I started the deposition of each parent with very general questions, and only on the second day did I even get close to the topics Putnam and I were actually most interested in. There were a number of interesting findings, but there was one particular response of Mrs. Doe's that absolutely floored me. To the question, "Did Seth otherwise ever breach your trust in any way prior to the night of your discovery?" she answered with an emphatic "no." I looked up at her to take in her expression, but all I found was an ice-cold blank stare.

We took a break at this point, and the conference room quickly emptied as everyone headed to the restrooms or the firm's coffee room. Only the court reporter stayed behind to fuss with a troublesome change of paper for her steno machine. I'd known her for years from scores of other depositions—in this and many other cases—and we typically spoke frankly with one another.

"I don't know about you, Ruth, but if my home life as a child had turned on one single infraction, I would have been booted out of the family a hundred times."

"What do you mean?" she asked without looking up, deeply involved in her struggles with the complicated-looking machine.

"Well, hell, when I was a boy, I misbehaved right, left, and center. I'm probably the only adult you know who remembers the name of his grammar school principal: Sandra Jenkins. I'd misbehave in a classroom and get sent to her office. Mrs. Jenkins would counsel me on how to handle myself, and I'd straighten out and fly right on whatever that particular issue was. But there were so many issues, so many ways to get in trouble. Childhood's not easy. I remember the time my dad found me lighting matches behind the garage. I had accidentally lit up a little pile of leaves. I must have been about six. He put the fire out, sat down, and took me in his arms. Sure he talked to me about matches and fires and being careful, but mostly he reassured me that everybody makes mistakes, and that the only thing you need to do in life is learn from your mistakes. Hell, this kid Seth didn't get that—you heard what the adoptive mother said. He hadn't given them any trouble on anything whatsoever for eighteen months. God, he must have been so careful and aware of what they wanted. And then he makes one false step—admittedly a serious one—and *BANG!* in an hour he's in a police squad car and his life ends. Poor kid."

"Ah, sorry," Ruth said, finally looking up, clearly relieved at having straightened out the problems with her equipment. "What were you saying?"

As if on cue, the dozen other attorneys began wandering back into the room, and O'Toole and his client were soon seated and the deposition resumed. Now it was time to approach the touchier topics, beginning with whether or not the Does felt comfortable talking about sexual matters with other adults. I questioned whether their long service in the Catholic Church had made them in any way ill at ease with sexuality in general, and even asked them about the pattern of sexuality in their own marriage. On and on I went, accomplishing nothing, with the exception of embarrassing the hell out of everybody in the room.

Then, in utter desperation, I suppose, I took a wild gamble at almost the very end of the second day of Mrs. Doe's deposition. My question, which wasn't even written in my outline, was based on nothing more than a statistic Putnam had once mentioned to me years before in a different law case: fully a quarter of women in the United States experienced some form of sexual mistreatment as children. As I said, completely on a whim, I quoted this statistic and simply asked the deponent if she was among that group. Twenty seconds of silence followed, during which Mrs. Doe's face became progressively more flushed and increasingly stranger sounds welled up from her throat. And then she suddenly exploded into a storm of tears and bawling. She struggled to regain her voice, and of course, we all waited patiently while she took one deep breath after another in her effort to regain her composure. Finally, she looked up, ready to proceed. Glances shot back and forth between the defense attorneys, several of whom had been borderline asleep before this turn of events.

"Yes, I was, actually," she said in a strong voice that was half an octave lower than we had heard in her previous testimony. I was fumbling for a follow-up question, but I didn't need one. She was off and running. "My older cousin touched me when I was just about Ashley's age. He did this repeatedly when our families were visiting my grandmother's house, which we did on Sundays every other week. He and I were supposed to be helping out by vacuuming, but he used the vacuum noise to cover up . . . to cover up his . . . his . . . abuse." Her words once again deteriorated into loud sobs and moans that came from deep down within her. I asked her if she wanted to take a break, but in response she held her right hand up and vehemently shook her head no. It took her a good two minutes to gain enough control over her voice to ask for a few more moments respite. Then, still without another question from me, out came the nugget that the panning gold miner finds after sifting through half a mountain of streambed soil. "That's why I knew the night I walked in on them how violated Ashley must have felt, and why we had to get Seth out of her life right then, that night, immediately, once and for all. That's why I called the police, and that's why I insisted that we end Ashley's misery *immediately*. That boy needed to be dead for her—gone forever. She didn't need to be tortured by his presence the way I was by my cousin until he finally moved to California years later when we were adults."

Complete silence filled the room when Mrs. Doe finished. I looked over at Attorney O'Toole, who was looking right at me. He had a small, sly smile on his face, and he almost imperceptibly nodded at me. Clearly he considered this surprise testimony helpful to his case, and I could only surmise that to him it seemed further evidence of how vulnerable and fragile Mrs. Doe had been and how much damage had been done to her by the defendants' negligence. I thought it ironic that I too was thinking about how my case would benefit from what had just been revealed. From my perspective, the testimony showed that the adoptive mother had been far more fixated on herself and her personal history that fateful night than on what was best for Ashley and Seth.

Later that evening, Putnam's booming voice filled the phone line when I told him what Mrs. Doe had disclosed. "I knew it! I fucking knew it!" he called out. "That explains so much to me. Hang on, I want to make a few notes in the record." A good three minutes of silence followed, and then he came back on the line. "So how good is this disclosure for you on the legal end of the case?"

"It's a gem. Trust me. It's a gem." I found myself smiling as I said this, not that I took lightly Mrs. Doe's trauma and suffering; not at all. She had every right to do what she needed to do for herself as a survivor of her cousin's sexual predation. But in my view, that needed to be distinguished from whether or not it was appropriate for her to make a rash decision that fateful night with Seth and Ashley, and to do so without any professional consultation as to what was best for the children.

We were now a year and a half into the case, and on a dazzling, sunny day, the first deposition of the children began. Each child was scheduled to be deposed over three full days, which meant the process would stretch over six consecutive Tuesdays.

At the end of each of these six days, after the stenographer had packed up and left the room, the eleven defense attorneys typically stayed for at least another half hour to confer on what had been learned and what it all meant and implied. Several things were universally agreed on by each and every one of us, and hence seem well worth reporting. First, we were enormously impressed with how bright and articulate the children were. These were extremely well-spoken, thoughtful teenagers, who seemed well beyond their years in many ways. But we were also struck by the depth of character of each child. They were captivating, even charming. Besides having remained as strikingly good-looking as ever, there was a warmth and a quiet strength to both personalities. We were really, truly impressed—all of us—and it's got to be hard to fool an entire room full of clever people.

But we also all commented on the fact that the children were beginning to show the effects of the constant wear and tear on them from everything they'd been through, including the stress of the litigation. And, not surprisingly, there was an element of underlying sadness in each of them. How could there not have been with all the loss and separation they had endured? But even here there was balance. Something had instilled in each of these children an element of brightness that somehow had not been extinguished—not yet anyways.

On the second day of Ashley's deposition, I began to inquire about what losing Seth meant to her. She was open and honest in answering. She told us that she had been completely devastated by the loss of her brother, which she testified her adoptive parents had told her was "necessary" and "permanent." When asked at what point she had heard them say this, she was very clear. They had told her this immediately after the police had marched Seth out of their house that calamitous night. She said she missed Seth terribly, even now, and, as she phrased it, "I know that somehow we will find each other later in life." When she said this, she crossed her arms over her chest and gave herself a little squeeze. This was body language I very much intended to communicate to Putnam.

When the defense team discussed Seth after his deposition, we all agreed that we perceived him as a disheartened boy run down by life. But again, it was not so simple, because we also found that there was still a remarkable warmth to this handsome boy and elements of resilience and optimism to his character. His remaining hopefulness, however, ran smack into the sad daily life he endured in the sexual offender program to which he'd been condemned. Living in a secure facility, he was, in effect, a prisoner, whose every movement was monitored and restricted. And his adjudication had formally branded him as a sexual offender. This meant his name was entered into the Massachusetts Sex Offender Registry, the consequences of which are staggering. It's nearly impossible for registered offenders to find a job or rent an apartment because employers and landlords have open access to the registry.

Seth testified that he was trapped between the horns of a terrible dilemma, given his refusal to admit to his clinician that he was a sex offender. Apparently nothing had changed since I had first heard about his life in the offender program.

He confirmed that the consequences of insisting on this had been made clear to him prior to his decision. No admission meant he would be treated as being in denial of his compulsion disorder, which in turn meant he couldn't even *begin* climbing the behavior modification ladder that would have eventually led to his being trusted to live in an unlocked facility. And so, month after month, he remained at the bottom of the hierarchy, enjoying no privileges at all. When I probed the matter with additional questions, Seth testified that he would never make the required admission, no matter what the cost to him.

"I didn't rape my sister," he asserted. "That's not at all what we were doing together. They don't understand. I would rather stay as a level-one offender than to accept their definition of what I did, of who I am."

Seth described life in the birth home as isolated and insular. He reported that neither he nor Ashley had neighborhood friends of any consequence and that this was in significant part because of how adults in the household presented the world. Seth testified that his father (who was also his step-grandfather) repeatedly reminded the children that there was their "family and its ways, and there was the outside world and its ways." Both children stated that they had been brought up to never, ever talk to anyone outside the family about life inside their household. The children's father was apparently quite adamant about the importance of "keeping everything that happened in our house private, because other families would never understand, and because other families have their private ways too."

The details of the ritualized sexuality that was imposed on the children, especially by their father/step-grandfather but also by their grandmother, uncle, aunt, and mother, were well known to all counsel from the police report and prosecutorial record. These details were so shocking, in fact, that they made it nearly impossible for most of the defense attorneys listening to the testimony to grasp why the children still spoke with such affection for their birth family. But the truth is, there was complete consistency between the two siblings on the issue. Both still cared deeply about their birth family, notwithstanding all that had taken place in their home and the devastating consequences that ensued. The heart and soul of the testimony given by the two siblings on this issue can be summarized as follows:

First, both children made it clear that they now fully understood the criminality and gross impropriety of the sexual assaults of the adults in their home. It was obviously very important to each of them to articulate this point. Seth brought it up three different times.

Second, each child was literally pleading with us to try to understand that they had depended on their parents, just like any other child does. You literally could have heard a pin drop in the conference room when each child set out to convince us that while there was what they now understood to be illegal and impermissible sexuality, there was also an abundance of love and nurturing in the household. Seth, who was both older and more articulate than his sister, tried as hard as he could to get us to recognize how the family's physical touching— sometimes sexualized, sometimes not—was to him and his sister "simply life as we knew it" (his term).

"It wasn't like they were trying to hurt us," he told the attorneys. "You need to understand that. I've heard stories in my offender program about parents who intentionally hurt their children. There's nothing in common. One boy has dozens of round scars on his back from cigarette burns because that's how he was punished. Our parents never, ever hurt us. They just didn't know or care that you had to keep grown-up ways of sex away from your children. They got that part all wrong, completely wrong. But that's different from not loving us, and it's very different, totally different, from hurting us on purpose." Each time Seth finished these little lectures, which he would append to answers to my questions, he would look around the table of attorneys for approval, or at least acknowledgment of what he had said. But every time this happened, with the exception of yours truly, he only encountered blank stares or the tops of heads of attorneys madly writing in their note pads.

I asked Seth a series of questions aimed at trying to learn what regular games the children played inside their new home and what they did outside on the large grounds. He listed a dozen board and other games and described a number of imaginative outside games the siblings played together. But when I asked whether their sexual couplings were possibly a form of play for them, Seth adamantly rejected this characterization. So did Ashley in her deposition. I had to admire the strength of character it took for each of the children to refuse to buy into even a friendly effort to impose an external definition on their sexualized behavior. So if it wasn't sex, and it wasn't sex-play, what was it? It was time to learn the details.

I asked each of the children when and how they were together sexually, and both reported that it would only happen late at night when one would awaken and go quietly into the other's room. Then, while trying to be as delicate as possible, I elicited what the children actually did together. The response from both was given without hesitation or embarrassment. The sexuality amounted to hugging, kissing, stroking, and, indeed, vaginal penetration. As gingerly as one can, I asked Seth if he ejaculated at any time, and consistent with the fact that he had not yet been through puberty when he lived with the adoptive parents (and also consistent with Putnam's theories on the matter), he answered, "No, I was too young, and that just wasn't in my mind. That wasn't the point."

Ashley said the same thing in her deposition. When I inquired who went more often into the room of the other, they each reported that it didn't matter, that it could be either one of them. They both said this took place about two or three times a week.

Seth gave fascinating testimony in response to questions seeking to elicit *why* they had sex together if it wasn't sex and it wasn't sex-play—especially because after the destruction of the birth family home, they knew perfectly well that there were serious consequences to incest.

Seth gazed off into the distance while thinking about his answer, and then, after a good thirty seconds, he told us, "When I was holding Ashley, it was . . . how I got back to my family. It was as if I could actually feel and hear and smell the family all around me again, like when we had dinner with everyone sitting around the table eating and laughing. In the adoption house, everything was formal and dry. There wasn't any laughter, there wasn't any nonsense, and there weren't any smells—just the smell of soap and those spray cans. But at my parents' house, it was completely different. It was loud, and crazy, and funny, and it smelled good. Once my dad spilled spaghetti sauce on his clean shirt, and after he looked down at the mess, he looked up and said how stupid he felt. We always put on clean shirts for dinner, but you know what we did? Every one of us started smearing spaghetti sauce on our shirts too, and then all over our cheeks, and we all laughed so hard and so long that we all had tears running down our cheeks making tracks in the spaghetti sauce."

Telling this made Seth laugh out loud, and he looked around the table at the twelve attorneys to see if anyone would share the moment with him. He found only one big smile; with all my heart and soul I wanted to call out, "Hell, why don't I get invited to parties like that?" but with the stenographer taking down every word, I refrained. Now, of course, I wish I hadn't.

Anyway, Seth sighed and then turned his head away, looking off into space again, inner space probably, and continued his answer without another prompt from me. "Can you lawyers *possibly* understand what I'm saying?" With these words, another sad sigh came out, all on its own. "When I held Ashley in the adoption home, I could actually feel again how much my stomach hurt from laughing so hard on the spaghetti sauce night. I could see everyone around the table, real clearly. With my everyday memory, I was starting to lose the faces. I don't have any photographs, you know. I could smell my home again when I held Ashley, but I can't smell it usually. Anyway, that's what it was like at my real home. You were constantly bombarded with feelings and sights and sounds and smells. I know it must sound crazy to you, but when I held Ashley it was like a way back to all that. It wasn't just memories that came back to me when we were alone together; it was the feelings and the sounds and the smells *themselves.* And it was the same for Ashley, because when we were in bed together, we talked about how weird it was to have it all come back so clearly. Sometimes, we'd lie there holding each other, and we would share some memory that would crack us up, and we'd have to put the pillow over our faces so we wouldn't make noise."

I had no further questions for Seth, and this answer concluded his deposition. There is no way I can describe how profoundly silent the room was after Seth finished speaking. The sound of that silence has stayed with me ever since.

In Ashley's final day of deposition, when I asked her what the sexuality with Seth meant to her, she looked down at the table for a long time, and then began to answer in such a quiet voice that the court stenographer had to ask her to speak up. We were completely mesmerized. At one point, she used a metaphor I will never forget: "It was like drinking water when you're really, really thirsty." Ashley told us that as far back as she could remember, she had always been held and kissed and touched and loved by everyone in her family. She testified that, "Even though I learned that the sexual parts of the loving were very, very wrong and illegal for families to do together and for kids to be involved in, in some ways I missed it, and in some ways I was thirsty for it. Seth and I had this beautiful secret—a secret that came from our real family. And it was so powerful we couldn't resist it. And we couldn't resist it even though we knew our adoption parents would never, ever understand if they caught us. But when I woke up at night and was scared by things or sad at my mom being so gone, it was Seth I wanted to be with, not my adoption mom. I mean she tried hard back then to be a great mom, but she couldn't possibly understand. It was like Seth and I had a secret place to go to that only we knew about. And it was only when we were together in bed and touching each other that we ever talked about home. And it was more than just talk. It was like we were back there in our house." This final sentence of Ashley's deposition was spoken slowly, with her eyes closed, her head gently turning from side to side.

As I drove home that evening after the sixth and final day of those depositions, I ran into the single most colossal traffic jam I had ever been in. At one point, it actually took me an hour to go half a block. While I was as frustrated as everyone around me, the enforced time alone ended up being a blessing in disguise. It gave me the perfect opportunity to process what an amazing experience I had been through in deposing these two children. Each had testified so willingly and openly about everything he or she had been through, and each had done so without any evident shame or remorse. It was as if they realized that this would be one of the few times they would *ever* be able to speak so candidly about the details of their lives in their two homes.

Sitting there in that interminable traffic allowed my mind to wander, to try to summarize for myself what I thought about the children now that I had come to know them in person. Most importantly, I realized that I truly believed Seth and Ashley when they testified that their parents raised and

nurtured them in a loving way. That's the only possible explanation Putnam and I could come up with as to why they survived so intact. But now, more was clear to me. I think for the
first time I realized that love is not enough, not in this family,
maybe not ever. These parents violated one of mankind's most
universal norms—the incest taboo—and the consequences for
these children were devastating. When you raise a child, it's
not okay to live solely within the bubble of love between parents and child, to live as if your home were the world. If it were,
then I suppose you could do it any way that works for you and
the children. But it's not just about you and your child and your
home. A parent's task is to raise a child so that they fit into the
outside world, not just into the idiosyncrasies of their nuclear
family. It follows that one of the principal duties of a parent
is to teach their child the norms and proscriptions of the culture and society in which he or she will live. Loving parenting,
I realized that day in traffic, cannot be selfish parenting, and
that was one thing the Doe children surely suffered: massive
parental selfishness.

About two weeks later, I received the final transcripts of
the children's depositions from the court reporter. I immediately messengered copies of all six of them to Dr. Putnam, but,
somewhat surprisingly, I didn't hear back from him. Just about
a month later he began his psychiatric examinations of the
children, which took place over a three-week period. Again, he
didn't call. Then one day, roughly three months after I had sent
the transcripts over, I received by messenger Putnam's final
written report.

I needed to be alone with the report, so I left the office,
as a busy law practice is essentially a series of incessant inter-
ruptions. And besides, it was only a short walk from my office
to several benches set at the water's edge on Boston Harbor—
exactly where the Tea Party events had occurred two hundred
years earlier. It was a remarkably warm late spring day, just

about two years out after the *Doe* case had arrived in the office. The sky was crystal clear, and the harbor water was as blue as a child would paint it. I plopped down on one of the benches and dove into the document; even the call of seagulls and the horns of passing ships failed to interrupt my concentration on Putnam's subtle and fascinating analysis.

It was the good doctor's opinion that there had been two principal moments of traumatic impact on the children. First, he reviewed what we knew about the birth home, along with the accidental disclosure and emergency removal of the children. During this first period, Putnam explained, based on the evidence in the written record and his corroboration of that evidence during his examination of the children, it was his considered opinion, "to a reasonable degree of medical certainty," that great and irreparable psychiatric harm was done to the children. But here was the unexpected twist: the psychiatric harm done during this period was, in his opinion, more a function of the sudden and final termination of the affective, emotional relationship between the children and their birth family than of the incest itself.

In parallel fashion, with respect to the period of time at the Does' house, Putnam's opinion was that the sudden disappearance of all that had been built between the children and the adoptive parents was a far more powerful stressor on the children than the prepubescent, mutual soothing these two siblings engaged in with their intersibling trysts. From the point of view of the children, Putnam wrote, the transition from their humble origins to the luxurious setting of the Doe household was like a Cinderella story. Imagine, Putnam implored, the psychological cost for a child to make this sociological transition and then to lose it all in an hour. And, the analysis continued, if Seth's loss of the new life he had come to know at the Does' palace was great, Ashley's loss of Seth's love and company was even greater.

In discussing the intersibling sexuality, Putnam developed a fascinating metaphor. Think of the children, he suggested, as if they were bilingual adopted siblings who, when they were alone together, spoke to each other in the language of their birth home. Actually, this would be expected, and it's hard to imagine that an adoptive parent would fail to respect this or tell the siblings to stop speaking in the second language. And, he pointed out, modern-day adoption protocol for parents in international adoptions strongly encourages adoptive parents to learn what they can of their adopted children's native tongue and to take the child to visit their country of origin, if feasible. With all this in mind, Putnam urged, think of the body language between Ashley and Seth as analogous. The sexualized touching they engaged in was a reproduction of the body language they had used in their birth home. His opinion went still further. He advocated that we see the late-night, prepubescent couplings in the adoptive home as more ritual than sexual. These children, he wrote, were desperately lonely and entirely adrift. They were cut off from their roots with devastating finality, and for purposes of dealing with this loss on an emotional level, they had only each other, and in these late night moments they spoke to each other in their native language—sexualized touching.

Putnam also wove into his analysis a series of additional potent stressors that he thought had done harm to the children. These included Ashley's anger with her adoptive parents for their abandonment of Seth, Ashley's guilt at seeing Seth criminalized for their mutually-initiated sexuality, and interestingly, Ashley's quiet rage over being forced to relive all of this in the process of the lawsuit itself. The last of these was something he had picked up in his psychiatric examinations that I had missed altogether in my deposition inquiries.

The conclusion, accordingly, was that by far the greatest stressors on the children were the two sudden and brutal losses of family connections. These psychological insults, Putnam summarized, were of an altogether different magnitude than were the sexual deviancy of the birth home and the intersibling sexuality of the adoptive home.

When I finished reading Putnam's report, I put it down on the bench beside me and just let the fresh air, the seaside sounds, and the beauty of the afternoon wash over me like a shower. I remember now that my mind wandered that day, for some inexplicable reason, to an image of my son's recent little league baseball game, during which he had slid headfirst into a very dusty home plate. He had been on first base when the next player hit a pretty hot grounder. These were just little guys, and at their age, this particular grounder, like most others, eluded both the shortstop and the left fielder. By the time the kid in left field had retrieved the ball and tossed it to the shortstop, my boy, having completely ignored his coach's signal to stop at third base, was heading full speed ahead for home plate. Six-year-old shortstops don't throw very hard, so the ball sailing home and my son could be seen racing each other at roughly the same speed. And they arrived at home plate at precisely the same moment. The commotion of the headfirst slide and the catcher's tag threw up such a huge cloud of dust that both kids were invisible for a few seconds. The parent serving as umpire stood over the tangled-up players waiting for the dust to settle, and I stood in the stands alongside my aged father who was visiting from out of state, hoping against all hope for the call to go my son's way. And it did! "SAFE!" yelled out the umpire for all to hear. My son, still lying with his chest on home plate, looked up at the stands for his visiting grandfather and proud father, and when he found us, his dust-covered face broke into the toothiest smile I've ever seen. All this family stuff, as unimportant as it is in the great arc of human history, is not at all unimportant to the family members who live it. And that's what was lost to Seth and Ashley, lost forever. By the way, the coach ended up giving the game ball to my son, who signed it in his childish scrawl and gave it to my father. It was on my father's coffee table for the rest of his life. I found it there years later when I went to clean out his modest little house after he died, and it made me cry. I cried for the beauty of intact intergenerational bonds that that baseball represented, and I cried for the tragic loss of family connections I had come to know in the *Doe* case.

*

About three weeks later, Putnam and I met at his office with the goal of beginning the process of selecting a line of argument to present to the jury. The massive amount of data we possessed on the children was a treasure trove from a research point of view but daunting from a trial strategy perspective.

Putnam launched right in. "I am prepared to testify that, from a mental health angle, both of these children currently exhibit intact mental health. That's the shocking fact here. They're really quite impressive. Somehow they've survived everything they've been through. I'm amazed, really. One thing's for sure: there doesn't appear to have been any fear generated by the children's father or by the boundaryless sexuality in the birth home, and I probed hard for that. On the contrary, there's *still* a deep attachment to the birth family, and a heartfelt concern about the fate of their mother."

We were both quiet as we considered this anomalous case. "Rick," I finally asked, "how in the hell are we going to explain our case to a jury?"

"Oh, I've got a theory all right," Putnam came back with. "I've been piecing it together, as best I can. The police and prosecutorial reports are clear: the birth mother was young, and also young for her age, pretty much a child herself. The children told me she was as dependent on the grandparents as they were. And from what I could tell, they don't blame her in any way for what took place in the household, nor for what this led to. So what we have here, I think, is a case of 'parentified' children: kids who perceive the vulnerability of their parent, and do whatever they can to care for their parent's welfare. So part of the explanation as to why these children are so intact may be that they saw themselves as *needing* to keep themselves intact so they would be strong enough to keep their mother safe. This parentified-child phenomenon is not all that rare; we see it all the time in war zones."

"Okay. But how does this play into what you said a few minutes ago about the absence of fear? Why wouldn't children forced into caring for their incompetent parent experience fear at having to play such an exaggerated role in navigating the adult world?"

"Good question," Putnam replied, pointing at me sharply with his index finger. "I think the answer to that lies in what their father-slash-step-grandfather was like as a person. I examined the kids about him as closely as I could and from every angle I could think of. But *not once* did they ever express any fear of him—none whatsoever. I can't exaggerate how atypical this is for intergenerational family sexual abuse. Somehow, despite the persistent sexuality that he visited on these children, and despite his instructions to keep the family secrets from the outside world, something about the framework of the overall experience kept it from traumatizing the children. Fear played no role; that, I can guarantee you. Did you pick up any signs of trauma reaction in the kids in your depositions?"

"No, and neither did the other defense counsel. The eleven of us discussed it over and over again. To a person, we agreed: these children were intact, intelligent, articulate, even charming. And when they talked about the sexuality in the household, there was nothing in their language or body language that reminded me of the scores of survivors of childhood sexual abuse their age who I've worked with in other cases. To me, frankly, other than the content of their story, I would have never picked these children out to be survivors."

"So that's a dozen of us with the same reaction. And I was looking for all sorts of collateral clues: whether or not their memories were expressed in somatic or intellectual terms, whether or not their body language conformed to what they were saying, whether or not there were inconsistencies in their two stories, and whether or not what they told me was consistent with what the record shows they told clinicians and police authorities early in the case. And, don't forget, there's important corroboration for this in the fact that *not one* of their teachers or doctors or any other adult picked up any clue of a problem in the birth home until the accidental disclosure with the anatomically correct dolls."

"Yes, and I've got something else for you," I broke in, somewhat excitedly. "We've now deposed every single teacher, school counselor, and doctor we could still locate and I asked each and every one of these professionals to look back with twenty-twenty hindsight and tell me if they could now think of *any* hint of the sexuality they had missed at the time. And every single one of them answered no. Every single one, Rick. Not *one* of them even dreamed of the incestuous sexuality in the birth family home. How in the hell do you explain that?"

"That, my friend," Putnam said in his stentorian voice, "is because there was, as I said earlier, *no fear involved.* This is in total contrast to the kids I normally see in my trauma center—many of them live in fear twenty-four-seven. One thing I feel sure about—and this I can sure as hell tell your jury—the critical difference with the Doe kids is that the participation of these children with the ritual sexuality and their total compliance in maintaining the wall of secrecy was certainly not fear based. I'm convinced of that. That's why they gave off no signs or signals; I'm sure of it."

"So if their complicity wasn't fear based, what was it? Why such perfect compliance?" I wondered aloud.

"I don't know, to be honest with you. But I expect it's because they loved their crazy family, and because they felt safe and connected. Those are the key words, Terry. Safe and connected. And let me add this. My research is showing that just as traumatic memories are stored somatically and not intellectually, love memories are as well. That's why when you hear a love song from your teenage years, you can immediately picture the girl you were dating at the time. So if my theory is right, just as fear-based abuse or trauma is linked in memory to body sensations—the war vet who hears a car backfire and re-experiences the trauma he endured in combat—so love-based memories are similarly linked to body sensations. I think that's why these kids brought up *sensations* when you probed them about their memories of home: the *tastes* of Grandma's cooking, the *sounds* of dining room laughter, the *sights* of the spaghetti stains. Fear-memory and love-memory are stored in the brain stem, and linked to perceptions, as opposed to rote memory—the list of US presidents or whatever—that are stored elsewhere in the brain. There are two very different kinds of memory involved. These kids experienced the family sexuality as an integral part of the pattern of how their crazy, deviant family loved and connected with each other. My guess is that these children did not experience the need for secrecy as a threat about their abandonment but as a confirmation of their inclusion. Their family was a secret society, and they saw themselves as full members. My guess is that these children probably grew up thinking very little about their family's sexuality. From the perspective of the children, since they felt safe, nurtured, and loved at home, and since they were never physically or emotionally mistreated, the entire topic may have had much less importance for them than we as adults are likely to conceive."

"Okay, assume you're right," I followed on. "What would have been the implications for the children's mental health if there had never been a disclosure? Where would all this have come out in the end?"

"Oh, another good question," Putnam said, once again pointing at me. "As they reached puberty, I imagine things might have changed pretty dramatically. But let's put this in perspective. Of the more than twenty percent of girls and fifteen percent of boys sexually abused as children in this country, the vast majority grow up to lead psychologically healthy, normal lives. Of course, it's true that a certain percentage of survivors lead lives that are enormously tormented by what happened to them as children. We know so little about why some children can tolerate such abuse while others are deeply traumatized. But I'm afraid the only honest answer to your question about where the Doe kids would fall on this spectrum is to tell you that the science of psychiatry would have to be a hell of a lot more advanced than it is today for me to do better than just take a guess. That's all it would be—an educated guess."

"All right. Let's move on then. What are you going to be able to tell the jury about the psychiatric implications for the children of how the adoptive family handled the discovery of the intersibling sexuality?" I asked.

"That's easier. My testimony will be that the psychiatric impact of the intersibling sexuality *itself* was minimal when compared to the parade of horrors that came to pass in the children's lives after the adoption disruption. In my opinion, the children meant no harm to each other and did no harm to each other. And I can tell your jury that, while the children are psychologically solid young people, the loss to the siblings of each other, on top of the loss of the rest of their family, will probably in the end be the single biggest stressor on their future mental health."

"It's that big?"

"It's that big."

"Wow. Okay. I hear you. Let me ask you another question, a hypothetical one. Say you were the family shrink to the adoptive parents the night of their discovery of the intersibling sexuality. Say you got a call in the middle of the night from your clients. They had just found these two kids in bed with each other, having sex. How would you have counseled them?"

"Oh man, I would have loved to have taken that call." Putnam leaned forward, rubbing his massive hands together. "To begin with, I would have insisted that the matter could not and should not be thought through in the middle of the night. Everybody needed to go to sleep in safe, separate rooms until the next day when we could all put our heads together and look at the options. That would have changed everything, in my view. If the adoptive couple had taken the time to look at the possibilities, it seems unlikely that they would have done what they did," Putnam asserted.

"How so? What would you have said to them the next morning?" I asked. "And remember, the adoptive mom had her own issues to deal with."

"I would have told them that I actually saw a wonderful opportunity for them. They could have used this discovery to become the emotional parents of the children. All they would have had to do was to handle the disclosure of the intersibling sexuality with love and tenderness. They had the perfect opportunity to help the kids get to normal—for which the kids would have been eternally grateful. Metaphorically speaking, those kids could have been sort of reborn into normal childhoods at that point, since everything would have come out into the open. And I'll tell you something else. I would have advised Mrs. Doe to get counseling to deal with her own abuse as a child. She clearly needs to work on her untreated trauma. But mostly, I would have stressed that what the children needed was education about when and with whom sex is appropriate. What the children clearly did *not* need in their lives were more police, more criminal courts, more loss, and more stigma. And finally, I would have bet the parents a bottle of wine—hell, a whole goddamn case of wine—that in the midst of this transition process, Seth on his own would have initiated a conversation about being ready to have his adoption legally finalized."

"So no police, no social service agencies?"

"Absolutely not. I would have advised them to handle this by themselves, as a family matter, supported by private clinical family therapy."

Putnam was silent for quite a while. Then he told me something he had neglected to say up to this point. "You know, each kid probed me to see if there was any way they could see each other, or even if they could learn about how the other was doing. The boy actually asked me if I couldn't make up a story about why I needed to see them together to better understand what went on between them. It was tempting—really tempting—to join him in a scheme. But I assumed the parents would have objected, and the whole thing would have been back in court. Not what the kids needed."

Putnam paused again, then started up, his honeyed, baritone voice spellbinding in its resonance. "One last thing that really moved me: after Ashley had described to me how much she missed her brother, I asked her *how* she missed him. She said, and I'm quoting from my notes, 'I try not to think about Seth, because when I miss him, I miss him with my whole body. It actually hurts, like when you have the flu and you ache all over.'" Putnam looked up at me for a response, but what was there to say?

It was time to leave, but I had one last, practical question. "Rick, we're facing a bit of a double-edged sword here. How are you going to reply on cross-examination if the plaintiffs' attorney says to you, 'Now, Dr. Putnam, for purposes of this question, let's assume you're right that the intersibling sexuality was driven not by sexual aggression on Seth's part, but by the two siblings seeking to nurture each other in the "language of their birth home," as you put it. If that's one way siblings from a sexually abusive home deal with the past, shouldn't the children's psychologists and social workers, and especially the adoption agency who placed the children, have warned the adoptive parents about this possibility?"

Putnam responded in the formal tone of voice he used in court when he testified. "Let me try to explain, ladies and gentlemen of the jury. Psychiatry and its allied mental health professions are fledgling sciences. We are just beginning to understand how human beings react to the stimuli in their environment. We all understand linear causality: hit a pool ball at the correct angle, and sure enough, the target ball will go in the pocket. But hit a boy, and it is not at all clear how he will react. He may act out by hitting smaller children, or he may become determined to be the type of adult who doesn't go around hitting people. So mental health professionals can never *predict* human behavioral reactions the way your question presupposes. All we can do is list past reactions that appear in the literature or that a clinician has seen. And intersibling sexuality is extraordinarily atypical. I've never run into it before in over thirty years of work in this field, nor have any of the colleagues with whom I've consulted about this case." He smiled over at me. "How's that for an answer?"

"Oh, that'll do; that'll do." I replied with a grin.

We spent another ten minutes on routine case logistics before the meeting ended. I thought more and more about what a tragedy it would be if this case didn't settle. On top of all her other issues, if the case went to trial, Ashley would have to hear Putnam's testimony on how her adoptive parents had let her down so terribly by their precipitous and self-centered decisions. She didn't need that.

*

The case dragged on almost another year, during which time Attorney O'Toole deposed Dr. Putnam and I deposed O'Toole's expert witness. The trial clerk of the court finally set a trial date, and I began the arduous process of preparing for trial. But then, out of the blue, just three weeks short of trial, O'Toole called and told me the plaintiffs wanted to make a serious effort to settle the matter. The settlement amount he proposed was shockingly modest. To this day, I have no idea exactly what motivated the plaintiff parents to take a very modest six-figure number and call it quits. But it was the right decision on their part, for numerous reasons.

Within a week, I had arranged a meeting with the other defense attorneys to discuss the settlement offer. My fellow defense counsel were elated. They almost universally felt the case was way too risky to try, given that it was completely dependent on Dr. Putnam's capacity to convince the jury of his interpretation of the meaning and impact of the intersibling sexuality. They feared that if the jury ended up being at all sympathetic to the adoptive parents, the verdict could be staggering. I was the odd man out, convinced we could win a defendants' verdict, if with disastrous effects on Ashley. A counteroffer was arrived at—funded almost totally by those insurance companies that were so anxious to avoid trial—and I communicated it to Attorney O'Toole. The following day, the plaintiffs accepted the counteroffer, two-thirds of which was placed in trust for Ashley, with the final third funding a trust for Seth. So after all this work, the case was resolved and done with, almost anticlimactically.

Needless to say, Rhonda Wilkins was ecstatic with delight at having to chip in so little to the settlement amount, and she gave me her ultimate compliment before hanging up in my ear. "You do fucking good work, Counselor. I just may give you another case someday." And equally needless to say, my client, Susan Sears, was elated that there would be no need to testify at trial—a proposition she had been dreading for over three years at that point.

I never heard anything more about Ashley or her adoptive parents, who partway through the litigation had sold their massive house and moved out to somewhere on the West Coast. The following year I again ran into the clinical director at Seth's sexual offender program and asked how he was doing, and the answer remained the same: wrong kid for the program. Three months or so after the settlement, I packed up boxes and boxes of documents and transcripts from the case to be shipped out to the law firm's off-site document storage and thought that was the end of my involvement with the case.

It wasn't.

*

Roughly five years after the *Doe* case settled, I received a call from the executive director of a small children's social service agency I had represented for years. This agency ran half a dozen halfway houses located in towns to the north of Boston, and one of them was having some friction with an abutting neighbor who had hired an attorney. I gave this attorney a call, and we agreed to meet on-site to try to resolve the issue.

The evening in question turned out to be unseasonably hot and sultry for late spring, when the light lasts well beyond nine o'clock. Opposing counsel was an entirely reasonable gentleman, and we soon had the small matter between the neighbors ironed out. The program director and I ended up sitting on the front stoop for a few minutes as the heat of day faded into a delicate evening breeze.

I asked the director about the nature of the population of the boys in the house, and learned that they were sexual offenders who had done well in one of the three or four offender programs in the commonwealth. I was just saying good-bye when a young man came out and asked the director for the key to the game closet. She went in to get it, leaving me with the boy. I nonchalantly said hi, but instead of replying, he cocked his head to one side, as if trying to place me. I certainly did not recognize him.

"Attorney Freiberg?" he asked.

"Yes, that's me," I replied, completely puzzled as to how he would know my name.

"You don't recognize me, do you?"

"I'm sorry, I don't. Should I?"

"Maybe not. My name is Seth. You were the attorney for the adoption agency that placed me and my sister for adoption, and there was the whole lawsuit thing."

All of it, all that we had been through, came back in a flash. "Oh my God, now I know exactly who you are," I blurted out. "You've grown and changed so much, I would never have recognized you."

"No problem. Hey, can we talk? I'd love to ask you a few questions. Are we allowed to talk about the case?"

I felt unmoored. But a settled case is a done deal, and given the circumstances, I couldn't see why or how there could be a problem. "I don't see why not. Where can we talk?"

"Um, this is not a good place, obviously."

"Are you guys allowed to leave the house to get an ice cream or something?" I asked. "My treat."

"As long as we're accompanied by an approved adult."

I checked inside with the program director, who immediately approved the idea when I told her that I had been involved in the litigation around Seth's adoption disruption. Seth, now six feet tall but still as blond as ever, showed me to the local sweet shop, which looked like it hadn't changed one bit since World War II. In fact, they still had the old, weathered hand-painted sign on the wall that had no doubt hung outside for many a decade: ICE CREAM: 5 CENTS. We each ordered a sundae, and then strolled across the street to a park bench that faced out over the pond near the town green. Neither of us spoke for quite a while, and I used the time to try to think through what I could and couldn't say to an opposing party after a case is settled. It was hard to think straight, though, because the dark chocolate sauce was so ridiculously good that it kept grabbing my attention from the matter at hand. I had to say something, though, so I just went with the chocolate sauce.

"This always happens to me," I opened the conversation. "Whenever I eat something I really like, I stop talking. My wife gives me all sorts of trouble about it, but I can't help it. It just . . . happens."

Seth laughed good-naturedly, "I know what you mean."

"You said you had a few questions," I said. "So shoot."

Without a moment's hesitation, Seth asked, "Do you know what happened to my sister?"

"Well, as you know, the lawsuit was settled, and some of the money was put aside in a trust for her and some for you as well. But that's all I know about her. I never had cause to hear anything further. Toward the end of the lawsuit, the family moved to the West Coast, but I never even knew which state. But I distinctly remember being impressed with how well she was doing when I saw her in her deposition. But that's old news; what, about five years ago now?"

"Yeah, about that. Do you think she misses me, or do you think she's angry with me?"

Now I started to become progressively more uneasy at the direction the conversation was taking. I was trying madly to think through whether there were limits to what I should say, even from a clinical point of view. Presumably Seth had had a lot of psychotherapy, and in all likelihood, his taking responsibility for what had happened between him and his sister was part of his treatment. I certainly didn't think I should risk blowing his clinical therapy out of the water with Putnam's hypothesis about the relative innocence of the intersibling sexuality. I hesitated just long enough for Seth to see right through me.

"Mr. Freiberg, I promise you—cross my heart and hope to die—that nothing you say to me today will ever be repeated. Who would I repeat it to? I literally don't know anybody who even knows I have a sister, let alone anyone who knows what happened, except you, and this is probably the only conversation I'll ever have with you. I give you my word of honor, no one will ever hear about this. *Please!*"

Seth's entreaty and his piercing stare cut through me. Then something inside my head just said, screw it. I wanted to talk to him about the case as much as he wanted to talk to me.

"Seth, your word of honor is good enough for me. And honestly, I have some questions myself. Let's see. As to whether your sister blamed you, the answer is a resounding no. The psychiatrist who examined you in his office—remember the office with the fireplace?" He nodded yes. "He told me that Ashley was very clear: she never felt forced to participate, and she sought you out as much as the other way around. What she reported was entirely consistent with what you had said, namely that what the two of you engaged in, you both did voluntarily. So as I understood things, she didn't at all blame you for what happened."

I could see the boy's shoulders relax. He turned back to his ice cream. Then, in a slow and even voice, he asked, "Was she sad that I was taken away?"

"Sad? Are you kidding? She was heartbroken. You were her only sibling, her best friend, and her last link to your family.

She had the adoptive parents, of course, and they seemed to mean well and to intend to stick by her and do their best. But it was you she loved."

I thought he would smile or acknowledge this information somehow, but he immediately asked, "Do you think I can contact her someday?"

"I suppose, once she is an adult and out of the adoptive parents' home, you could try. I don't think I would suggest trying before that. And maybe you should have someone facilitate the reintroduction, like a social service agency. That might be a good idea, Seth. They could help you locate her, and they could feel out the circumstances to see if she too wanted to reestablish contact—but I don't doubt that she would. That might be the best way to go about it."

"How would they find her?"

"After her twenty-second birthday, after she presumably will have finished her schooling and moved out of her parents' house and into her own life, a social service agency, or an attorney who works in the adoption field, might be able to help you. If you don't have any better way, feel free to give me a call and I'll see if I can help find the right person to help you."

"Okay, thanks. That would be great. But from what you saw, do you think she is probably doing okay?"

"That would be my guess, yes. That psychiatrist found both of you very 'intact' as he put it at the time. He was enormously impressed with how resilient both of you were, especially given everything you'd been through. And after your deposition, and also after Ashley's, the whole room full of attorneys talked about each of you, and we all had the same impression. You both had held it together remarkably well, and through some rough times. So I would imagine she is doing just fine. How about you? How are you doing?"

He paused, and looked me right in the eyes. "Do you really want to know, or are you just saying that to be polite?"

"No, I do really want to know. There is a lot I would like to know. I had no way to learn anything after the lawsuit ended, and it ended so abruptly."

"Okay," Seth said. "Ask me anything."

"Okay. Let's start with what happened to you in the Juvenile Justice System. I knew the basic details at the time, but what was it really like being in the system?"

"It was awful. Dreadful. At first, I was locked up in Roslindale; that's a prison for kids. Do you know it?"

"I do."

"Then they moved me to the sex offender program. That was better, but it still was a lockup, with super strict rules. I was sort of a little kid. I didn't know the first thing about how to defend myself or how to deal with these guys. And some of these characters were very hard on me. They were older, bigger, and streetwise. A few of them were very aggressive sex offenders, and that's what was on their mind." He paused, looking down at the ground. "Anyway . . . a lot happened. But I survived it, you know how?" he asked rhetorically. "Because I didn't care. I didn't have anywhere to go. I didn't have anyone to go back to. I didn't have any real parents or even adoptive parents—no sister, no friends, no home, no nothing. I really didn't care how they used me."

I was left wildly fishing for some way to respond to this. "Didn't you have *anyone* on your side, like a sympathetic social worker or a good program director? Maybe a teacher? How about the lawyer who did the case for you?"

"No, that lawyer disappeared at the end of the case. And I never lucked into having a social worker or a shrink who I really got to know. I kept getting social workers who quit. Every three or four months, I'd get a new one, and each one knew less about my case than the one before. And as time went on, each of them showed less and less interest in learning much about me. I was just a quiet kid who didn't cause any problems in the program. Maybe I should have. Causing trouble got some kids more attention. But that's not my nature. And with each new social worker, my file kept getting thinner and thinner. I always thought that was sort of ironic. Remember how fat my old file was? Not anymore. My current worker meets with me for about fifteen minutes and has no clue about my case. Mostly she just compliments me for behaving. No one knows, I swear, no one knows what you know about my background. No one. They only know from the folder that I'm a registered sex offender who stays out of trouble in the program and who has no visitors."

I had to think about what to ask him next. It took a few moments. "So how long can you stay in this halfway house?"

"Only about five more months. I'm in the system until my eighteenth birthday; then I'm out on my own."

"So that's cool. Are you excited about that?"

"No, not really. Not at all, actually. I'm too scared. A guy like me, with no education and no job skills . . . What the hell am I going to do?"

"Well, at least you have the settlement money. It must be safe and sound, and more by now. You could get a start with that, no?"

"Yeah, there's that, I suppose, although I haven't heard about it in years. The lawyer took a third of it, but there's an account somewhere. But that's not what matters. What matters is that I don't have anyone to call when I get out. No one at all to call or go see. No one."

Again, I was desperately at a loss for what to say. Seth noted this, I could tell, and let out a long breath that nearly broke my heart. "I'm lonely, man. Lonely to the point of being weary. And that's here in the program where at least there are a few people around me I can talk to. Once I'm out of here, I'll be even more alone. Then what do I do? Who am I even going to talk to then? Some stranger on the sidewalk? That's what really scares me. I hate being alone. Loneliness for me isn't an idea. It's a feeling, an awful feeling. Am I making any sense?"

"Yeah, you're making a lot of sense. You're saying things that are nearly the same as what Dr. Putnam told me during your case. One day he said something just like you said."

"Great. I'm a goddamn expert on loneliness. Maybe I'll write a book about it."

"Maybe you should," I replied.

"No, *you* should," Seth shot back. "You know how to write. I don't. And if you do, talk about my case, would you? Tell people what happened to me. *Please.*"

"Maybe I will someday. Who knows? Maybe I will. But I've got a question for you. When I feel hungry or thirsty, I start thinking about getting something to eat or drink. What do you do when you feel lonely?"

"What do I do?" He looked down at the ground again. "Mostly I go backward, back into myself. I try to refind the feelings that I had for my family when I was little, at home. But I can't really get back to them anymore, not since I lost Ashley. I know our home was nutty and what my family did was completely unacceptable, but I didn't know that then, or care. I was just a kid. What I search for now when I take walks back inside myself is what it felt like being part of my own big family, whether they were crazy or not. But now I just have a few vague memories. I can't get back to the feelings of family like I could when I was younger."

"But, Seth, you didn't really answer my question, and I really want you to. You said when you feel lonely, you mostly go backward to a time before you were alone. Do you ever think of going forward? Do you ever think about making new friends, new connections?"

He didn't hesitate. "I think about it, sure. But I can't really make friends while I'm in these programs. Kids come and go, and you're not supposed to talk about your background and personal stuff with other kids in the program. People who work here come and go. They burn out quickly and leave the job. Then in comes some complete stranger who doesn't know you and doesn't care. Maybe I'll be able to make friends, or find a girl when I leave here at the end of the year, but I don't think that's so obvious."

"Why do you say that?"

"Because when I turn eighteen in a few months and leave this program, what the hell am I going to do? I'm a registered sex offender. You're a lawyer; you know what that means. I'll have to report to the police wherever I live. You tell me: How do I get a job? From what I hear, employers check the registry. That's what it's there for. How do I rent an apartment? Landlords check the registry. That's what it's there for. Now you tell me: How do I make friends? Do I lie about my background? Do I just leave out where I've been for six years? And what will I tell a girl? Do girls date registered sex offenders? I don't think so. Or do I just not mention it, hoping they won't ask or learn? If I did keep it secret and they learned about it, they'd leave in a heartbeat, wouldn't you? But if I don't keep it secret, how do I explain what happened? Am I supposed to try to convince a girl that it was okay under the circumstances for me to have sex with my own sister? You tell me: What am I supposed to do?" There was such desperation in his voice, I wasn't at all sure how to respond or what to say next.

Seth was patient as I gathered my thoughts. But my mind was chaotic and not at all on topic. In a flash, what came to mind was the stark difference between my own eighteenth birthday and Seth's upcoming confrontation with adulthood. Mine was filled with excitement and anticipation. My dad took me on a little vacation to celebrate my high school graduation, and the University of California, Berkeley had by some miracle admitted me for September. I had had family. Seth had none. I had had education coming my way; Seth had none. I had had every reason to be elated and optimistic; Seth had none. I had had a whole range of connections to support my transition to adulthood; Seth had none. What to say?

The only option was to answer honestly. "I don't have any magical answers for you, Seth. I really don't. When I was your age, I had family and college and a future all mapped out for me. I know you don't have any of that. But you're a great guy. If I met you and were your age, I'd definitely want to make friends with you."

"Yeah, but you say that because you know I'm *not* a sex offender, because you understand what really went on between my sister and me. But no one else will understand that, *ever.*"

Once again I was frozen, trying to find something useful to say. "Well, what about that idea of reconnecting with Ashley when you're both adults. She'd understand."

"My shrinks have told me that she's probably gone forever to me because even if I could locate her, her shrinks and parents would probably advise her not to see me. And she may not want to. I'll bet you she tells people she's an only child. I wouldn't blame her." He paused and looked down at the ground. "It may be better for her if I don't ever show up again."

Now I was at a total loss for words. All I came up with was, "Look, that decision is years away. If you get your life up and ticking, who knows what the world will look like to you six or seven years from now. Have you ever asked an attorney or social worker about the ins and outs of getting your sex offender registration changed to a lower level?"

"Oh, sure, we talked about that. My best social worker—she got cancer and quit suddenly, wouldn't you know it—she told me two or three years ago that she called the lawyer for the Sex Offender Registry Board to see if there was an appeal process. She said the lawyer told her the board couldn't and wouldn't reconsider my registration status until at least ten years after my adjudication and that, in all likelihood, I would probably have to wait the full twenty years until my duty to register would end automatically. That's fifteen years from now." He went silent, back into his own thoughts for a moment. "You know what? She was really cool, that social worker, because it was after she got sick and had to quit her job that she followed through and took the time to call me at the program to tell me about all this. What a cool lady."

"It doesn't get a lot cooler. I hope to hell she's okay."

"She died actually, not that long after."

How to continue? I had no idea. What came out was, "So how's it going for you here at this program? Is there any way I can be of help? I've been their lawyer for years."

"It's fine here these days. I don't have any complaints. But when I turn eighteen, like I said, I'll have to leave, because my funding stops. But where do I go? What do I do? Do you have any ideas?"

I thought for a moment. "What about going to school? You're obviously smart. And you've got money in your trust."

"School? Based on what? I had essentially zero education in the two foster care homes, and then I had a year and a half-year of remedial work when I was in the adoptive home, and I was starting to catch up. But since I was arrested, I've had almost none. The offender program had a schoolroom on the campus, but it was a joke. Once I got in this halfway house, I wanted to go to the local high school, but with the sex offender registration, no dice. They have a teacher who comes into this program to teach two hours a day, but you can imagine the quality of the education. Kids of all ages are sitting there; some can't even read. So you tell me: How do I get out from behind the eight ball and get a real education? I read fine, but I have no historical knowledge or scientific understanding of how things work—nothing that takes a teacher and a classroom to learn."

I took out a business card and handed it to him. "Listen, you keep my card, and for God's sake, Seth, *you call me.* And call me with time to spare so I can help you generate ideas. Nobody eighteen years old should be left completely on his own. It isn't right."

"Okay," he murmured, looking down at the ground.

"Seth, I mean it. Call. I have resources and contacts, and who knows, maybe I can help you find a job and a place to live. You have your whole life in front of you. Don't give up. You've survived so much, and you've stayed so strong through all of it. You've done harder. Trust me: it *will* get better."

"But what hope is there?" Seth said, his voice choking up a bit.

"I'll tell you what, if you call me at my office, we will research if anything can be done to appeal to have your status changed at the registry. I'm sorry I can't tell you anything about the law on that issue today. I just don't know offhand how the registry works. But let's double check that your social worker got that right. And if we can make a try at it, I'd be glad to do it for you. And let me try to help you find a job and a place to live when you leave the program. I might fail, but I'll sure as hell give it a try. Will you call me?"

"Yeah," he replied, unconvincingly.

I wasn't going to let this go. "I'm serious, Seth. I care about how this turns out for you because I know all the details about how you fell into this trap, and I know it wasn't your fault. And don't tell anyone you're alone anymore, because I'll personally take that as an insult. You have at least one connection now—*with me.* And I promise you: I'll help you make five more connections. It's all about connections, Seth. Let's go make some."

To my complete and utter delight, as we both stood up from the bench, I saw a truly beautiful sight: a smile spread across his handsome face, only the second one I'd ever seen.

The short drive back to the group home was silent, but I sensed we both enjoyed the relaxed, quiet silence that comes over those who have said what they have to say. When I pulled up in front of the building, he looked at me and gave me yet another smile that I will never forget as long as I live as he told me "Thank you" in a deep and warm tone of voice. Then he opened the door and walked up the path toward the program's front door, without looking back.

There was no call the next week or the week after that. But I wasn't going to give up that easily, so I called the program director. She told me Seth was gone; he had run away from the program two days after I'd seen him, and had not been heard from since. I called his probation officer, who hadn't heard from him either. He told me that while that was normally a problem, since Seth was just about to age out of his probation status anyway, he didn't intend to do anything about it.

About a month later, I called the program again, but by then there was a new director who didn't even recognize Seth's name—or my name for that matter. I called the Division of Youth Services and found out who his case manager had been, but she was on maternity leave, and her replacement told me that she had never seen Seth's file. She promised to find the file and get back to me later in the week. And indeed, she dutifully did call back, but only to report that she had not been able to locate the file. Apparently it was lost. How ironic I thought: Seth had described how his file had shrunk over time, and now it was gone all together. Just like Seth's future. I thought about putting my private investigator on the matter, but I had to admit to myself the likely futility of this idea. And so I let myself get caught up in life, and let myself forget about Seth. Or so I thought.

*

The following winter, I had a court hearing in Salem, the next town over from where the group home where I'd run into Seth was located. After court, something made me drive over to the program, searching, I suppose, for some type of closure to the matter. I met the new director with whom I'd spoken. She was somewhat taken aback that the agency's attorney was at the door, unannounced.

"Don't worry; don't worry. I'm not here in any official capacity. I knew Seth, the resident I called you about a month ago. I knew him because I was one of the attorneys involved in a law case that grew out of his adoption disruption. I'm very concerned about him, frankly. I was hoping to give him a helping hand when he aged out of your program, but he never called. I was just wondering if you'd heard anything more about him since he ran from the program?"

"No. I've never even heard his name mentioned except by you on the phone when you called, and now again this afternoon. Actually, after you called, I asked several of the longer-term residents what they remembered about him, and they said they never had any real contact with him. They said they really didn't even notice when he left. They said he tended to keep to himself."

I thanked her, then turned and started down the walkway. I was halfway to my car when she called out to me from a window. "Hey, Counselor. You know what? There is a cigar box in a closet here that I think has his stuff in it. Do you want to see it? You're the only person who has ever asked after the boy. You can have it if you want. Otherwise, I'm going to throw it out."

I went back in and we opened the cigar box together in her office. The first thing I saw was my business card.

"Well, there you go," she said. "It's his box all right, and like I say, you're welcome to it."

Underneath the five or six random boy's treasures in the box was a photo. It was of the adoptive parents, Ashley, and Seth. But the photo had been mutilated: The parents' faces were both crossed out with blue ink. Ashley's face was crossed out with a black pen, presumably at a different time. And Seth's own face was crossed out with a third pen—a red ballpoint pen that was one of the items in the box. A cold chill ran up my spine and made me shiver, and inadvertently I made a funny little sound that somehow expressed the horror I felt at this discovery.

"What does all this mean?" she asked.

"What does it mean? It means, it's all about connections."

"What?"

"Oh, nothing, just an old saying. Hey, you take care. I have to get home. We have friends coming over to dinner."

*

My own words, *friends coming to dinner, friends coming to dinner, friends coming to dinner,* kept reverberating through my mind as I wound my way slowly through Friday afternoon traffic back to Boston. I couldn't get my mind off the lonely boy who was out there somewhere, presumably without friends, and quite possibly without dinner.

II

Loneliness and the Power of Permanency

AMY BANKS, MD

Arguably, nothing is more important to a human's physical and emotional well-being than a sense of belonging. But it goes further than that: belonging is a neurological necessity. People gather in supportive partnerships, families, and communities because human central nervous systems have evolved to develop and function most effectively and efficiently within groups. Our neurological lives literally depend on healthy interpersonal relationships.

While children and adults need relationships for support, comfort, and companionship over time, an infant *absolutely requires* healthy, responsive relationships with a parent or caretaker to develop the neural pathways needed for future connections. This means we need to ask ourselves: What are the neurological consequences for an infant when these relationships are absent? What happens neurologically to children who are raised in traumatic homes where sexual, physical, and emotional abuse is the norm? And what about children raised in families filled with other forms of extreme stress, such as domestic violence, severe poverty, or homelessness? What does it mean to the neurological development of a child raised in settings where the child's relationships with close adults are full of fear, insecurity, and worry?

Contemporary social service agencies now integrate this essential need for consistent relationships into their strategies for supporting healthy neural development of at-risk children. The term they use is "permanency," and a recent conference on this topic sponsored by The Home for Little Wanderers, at which this paper was presented, explored "The Power of Permanency" as one of the most important qualities in building support networks for children at risk. The power of permanency is twofold. On a concrete level, a child needs a permanent place to live, clothes appropriate to the climate, and nutritious food at regular intervals. Obviously, being sheltered from the elements and predators, and having a safe place to rest and relax, is crucial to a child's developing body and brain. But parental nurturing provides much more than warmth and safety to a developing child: without it, the child's sympathetic nervous system—which is activated during times of stress— runs twenty-four seven, keeping the child alert, on guard, and maximally stressed out. (If anyone doubts this, try watching a few episodes of *Naked and Afraid*!)

But shelter and sustenance are just the beginning. The power of permanency is equally important as an element in the relationships children have with nurturing adults as they grow and develop. Years ago, the famous psychologist Harry Harlow conducted a series of seminal studies on the impact of maternal separation on the rhesus macaque.[1] In these experiments,

---

1. Deborah Blum, *Love at Goon Park: Harry Harlow and the Science of Affection* (Cambridge, MA: Perseus, 2002), 225.

Harlow removed the infant monkeys from their mothers and then built surrogate mothers from wood and wire. In one experiment, he built two surrogates for the monkeys—one made of wire only but with a feeding bottle and then a second one with a cloth covering that gave the young monkeys some comfort when they attached to it. Repeatedly, he found that the monkeys preferred spending time with the soft cloth mother and only went to the wire monkey for feeding. Harlow argued that this was evidence that physical contact with a soft and caring other was as or more important than food. This was a remarkable and stunning finding. Other monkeys who were attached to the wire mothers alone without access to the softer, covered wiring, failed to thrive. Like our primate cousins, a child living on the streets may be able to beg or steal food—but he, too, will not thrive.

Relational-cultural theory takes the position that human development is always dependent on the presence of relationships: whether one is talking about the immature dependence of infants and children on adult caretakers—or whether one is referencing the mature, mutual interdependence exhibited by adults.[2] This theoretical model stands in direct contrast to earlier psychiatric theories that promoted separation and independence as the goals of both parenting and adult socialization. In these earlier models of development, humans were conceived of as being born dependent, with the goal of parenting and socialization being to mature the individual to a state of independence. In this paradigm, relationships are secondary. Caretakers are seen as little more than useful "objects" needed initially to give the nurturance required for a child to grow from a dependent childhood to a state of self-sufficient and autonomous adulthood. Popular advocates of this model, including Dr. Richard Ferber (let babies cry themselves to

---

2. Judith V. Jordan, *Relational-Cultural Therapy*, 2nd ed. (Washington, DC: American Psychological Association, 2018).

sleep) and Dr. Benjamin Spock (be a permissive parent), sold millions of copies of their books on how to raise children so they would *not* be dependent on others. Fortunately, in the last fifteen years, a new field known as "interpersonal neurobiology" has demonstrated the error in this line of thinking.[3]

Though a human baby is born in a dependent, immature state, it is endowed with all of the reflexes needed to connect. Much like a marsupial, a human child is born unable to fend for itself and requires, as argued above, the warm embrace of an adult caretaker in order for its nervous system to fully develop the relational capacities that will eventually allow the child to become a richly interconnected adult. Take, for example, the Moro reflex that allows an infant to cling to a mother. When I was studying pediatrics in medical school, I was assigned the task of conducting new infant exams. One part of the exam was to test for the Moro reflex by holding the baby over a bassinet and letting it drop a few inches back into my hands. A healthy child would let out a cry and extend its arms in front of its body in an arc as if reaching out for its mother. What this shows, is that being attached to a caretaker is so critically important to development that babies are born with this reflex to cling to a caretaker and to alert the mother with a cry when they are being separated. The physiological importance of this tactile connection with a parent cannot be overestimated, because throughout childhood, the holding and cuddling stimulate a release of important neurotransmitters from the brains of both parent and child. On one level, for both parent and child, the release of dopamine, norepinephrine, serotonin, and the endogenous opioids creates a felt sense of comfort and well-being in the moment of contact. But even more importantly, this process is *required* if the child is to succeed in building its neurotransmitter pathways into the

---

3. Daniel Siegel, *Pocket Guide to Interpersonal Neurobiology* (New York: W. W. Norton, 2012).

robust neural networks that will be needed later for the older child—and the adult he or she will become—to be capable of successfully connecting with others in its life.

Another reflex present at birth is the orienting reflex. This reflex causes an infant to follow a mother's smell and voice—presumably to help the infant stay closely connected to her. Still another reflex is the rooting reflex; it keeps a hungry baby searching for a maternal breast in order to sustain nutrition—and also to have the skin-to-skin contact that stimulates the development of the infant's neurotransmitter pathways. All of these rudimentary reflexes are present to facilitate and promote connection in infancy. But they do more than that: when a child is consistently responded to with love and nurturance, these reflexes develop into a rich neuronal network that will help the older child and adult that the child will become open up to and seek others for caring, concern, and sustenance.

*

The long-term impact of child abuse and neglect is staggering. The Adverse Childhood Experience Study has been looking at the impact of disrupted childhood bonds for over two decades.[4] Adults who had repeated stress in childhood from physical, sexual, or emotional abuse, or who came from broken homes, or who had a parent unable to care for them, have a 30 percent higher chance of developing heart disease, are twice as likely to be obese, and are 32 percent more likely to try to kill themselves. This is one of many studies that document the fact that dysfunctional parenting has long-lasting, serious health consequences.

---

4. Vincent J. Felitti et al., "Relationship of Childhood Abuse and Household Dysfunction to Many of the Leading Causes of Death in Adults. The Adverse Childhood Experiences (ACE) Study," *American Journal of Preventative Medicine* 14, no. 4 (May 1998): 245–58.

Over the past fifteen years, I have been following the research on how and why healthy connections are so important to the developing mind and body. In my book *Wired to Connect: The Surprising Link Between Brain Science and Strong, Healthy Relationships*, I describe four essential pathways for connection that are built and strengthened within healthy relationships during childhood.[5] While this is admittedly somewhat of a reductionist approach to the neurobiology of relationships—it does offer the reader a window into the importance of consistent, permanent connections in childhood. I use the pneumonic CARE to identify these pathways, with each letter standing for both a pathway and the characteristic the pathway provides in relationships. *C* stands for a feeling of **calm** that one gets when embedded in strong, healthy relationships and involves the functioning of the smart vagus nerve. This pathway—a recent addition to the nervous system (since the evolution of mammals)—inhibits the stress response when a person is safely connected. *A* stands for the **acceptance** and belonging one feels in a healthy relationship; this feeling of acceptance is dependent on the functioning of the dorsal anterior cingulate cortex (dACC)—a neurobiological alarm system that sends out a warning signal when we become disconnected from important others. *R* stands for the feeling of **resonance** that you have with safe others when your mirror neuron system is functioning well—this system allows you to read other people's actions, sensations, and emotions and feel a resonance with them. And finally, *E* stands for the **energy** or zest you feel in a healthy relationship and reflects the degree to which your dopamine reward system is firmly connected to healthy relationships.

---

5. Amy Banks and Leigh Ann Hirschman, *Wired to Connect: The Surprising Link Between Brain Science and Strong, Healthy Relationships* (New York: Tarcher/Penguin, 2016).

Dr. Jean Baker Miller, a psychiatrist and one of the founding scholars of relational-cultural theory, listed the "Five Good Things in a Growth-Fostering Relationship."[6] When a person is safely connected to another, he or she feels:

1. A sense of zest or energy
2. Clarity about himself, and the other person and the relationship
3. A heightened sense of self-worth
4. An increased ability to act both in the relationship and in the world in general
5. The desire for more healthy connections

When a person's four pathways for connection are robust and functioning well, these "five good things" are the normal, positive outcome of healthy relationships, and they act to protect the individual from stress-related physical and mental illnesses.

A closer look at each of these four neural pathways for connection can help explain how the "five good things" manifest themselves in healthy relationships. Additionally, understanding the neuroscience of connection explains how permanent, supportive relationships in childhood are crucial to the development of a child's neurological capacity to form complex, nuanced, mutual relationships as an adult.

When giving workshops on the CARE program explained above, I always start by asking participants to try a simple experiment that I call "Visualizing a Positive Relational Moment," a "PRM." The task is simple—imagine or visualize for one minute (and one minute only) a recent positive interaction you had with someone you feel close to. I ask participants

---

6. Jean Baker Miller and Irene Pierce Stiver, *The Healing Connection: How Women Form Relationships in Therapy and Life* (Boston: Beacon Press, 1997).

to shut their eyes as they replay the PRM interaction in their minds, and also to pay attention to what they are *feeling* in their bodies. I keep track of the sixty seconds and sit back and watch the crowd of people transform their expressions and body language into a new state that reflects the physiology of healthy connection. When asked to report their experiences to the group, the responses—regardless of whom I am talking with—tend to be quite uniform: an individual may report feeling a smile that came to his face, or an openness in his chest, or a relaxation of his shoulders. Another might report feeling a surge of energy, or happiness, or an ability to breath more deeply and feel calmer. At this point, I often punctuate the exercise by reminding people that one of the miracles of the human brain is the ability to transport ourselves back into these relationship moments anytime we want—and the value of doing so.

I follow this up by reminding people how often they feed themselves the memories of their last bad relationship moment—the time that they spoke too much, or were disrespected, or were left out. Not surprisingly, these negative or dis-connective experiences also change the participants' physiology: rather than feeling the embodiment of attachment, our internally retold negative relational stories stimulate our sympathetic nervous system, leading to feelings of stress. I encourage people to be intentional about what they are feeling in their brains and their bodies, and to remember how switching to a PRM can dramatically impact how they feel.

This ability to actively cause oneself to switch one's feeling from a negative relational experience to a PRM seems to be universal—although considerably less so for people raised in an abusive home, or a home where stress dominated the environment and safe relationships did not exist.

These sixty-second transformations in energy that can be achieved by visualizing a PRM seem mysterious at first, but they are less so if you think of humans as having evolved as pack animals. We can gain some insight into this line of thought by looking in greater depth at our four pathways for connection highlighted in the CARE program concept described earlier. In other words, I would like to examine whether or not the CARE model sheds light on the biological centrality of relationships for human development and ongoing health maintenance.

C, as you will remember, stands for the feeling of calm one gets in a respectful, mutual connection or interaction. The calm feeling emanates from the smart vagus nerve. Seminal research done by Dr. Stephen Porges at the University of Illinois revealed that during the evolution of mammals, there developed a third branch of the autonomic nervous system, the function of which is to modulate affect and behavior for the benefit of social relationships.[7]

When I was in medical school thirty years ago, I was taught that the autonomic nervous system is composed of two complementary branches—the sympathetic nervous system (SNS) and the parasympathetic nervous system (PSNS). These autonomic nervous system branches function automatically—beneath our level of consciousness—in response to the internal and external world in which we find ourselves. At baseline, SNS activation creates energy and activation to function in everyday life, while the PSNS takes over for periods of rest and rejuvenation. However, both systems have crucial roles when an individual is faced with a threat or with danger. When threatened, the SNS is responsible for the fight-or-flight response: energy, blood flow, and glucose are sent to the large muscles, the heart, and the lungs to help the individual prepare for and contend with the danger by either fighting or fleeing. When the threat becomes life-threatening and there is no longer the

---

7. Stephen W. Porges, *The Polyvagal Theory: Neurophysiological Foundations of Emotions, Attachment, Communication, and Self-Regulation* (New York: W.W. Norton, 2017).

opportunity to fight or flee, then the PSNS is activated, lead-ing to a closing down of biological systems and an outpouring of natural painkillers. In the extreme case, PSNS activation causes the individual to collapse and yield to the danger due to a shutting down of systems of the body. The individual can actually seem dead—protected to some degree from the pain of the attack by the release of endogenous opioids.

As described by Porges in his "polyvagal theory," the smart vagus nerve is part of a larger social engagement system whose role is to modulate the SNS and PSNS in the context of safe relationships. The smart vagus nerve and the social engage-ment system are composed of a number of cranial nerves (V, VII, IX, X, and XI). This system of nerves innervates the mus-cles of facial expression, the muscles in the throat and esoph-agus, and the tiny muscles in the inner ear. Polyvagal theory sees the autonomic nervous system as working hierarchically to respond to the environment depending on whether an indi-vidual feels safe, in danger, or in life-threatening danger. The ability to differentiate the level of safety in the environment is called "neuroception." When a person feels safe in the context of another, his face lights up, he smiles, his eyebrows raise, he vocalizes a response, he tunes in and listens more carefully. All of these behaviors activate the smart vagus nerve, which sends inhibitory feedback to the SNS and PSNS, telling each to stand down. Through this smart vagus input, interacting in a safe relationship literally leads to the physiological production of a feeling of calmness.

Neural pathways in the brain are created during childhood in response to the environment and then reworked through-out life. The developmental "goal" of the autonomic nervous system is to have each pathway accurately respond to the sur-rounding environment. If you are safe, you want your smart vagus nerve to kick in and de-stress you; in contrast, when you are in danger, you want your SNS to override the smart vagus and respond by priming you to either fight or flee. And, finally, if you are about to be attacked by a bear, you want the PSNS to take control to reduce the pain of your demise.

But take note that the development of complete and accurate neuroception is dependent on relational permanence during childhood. When a child is raised in an environment where basic emotional and physical safety is absent due to homelessness, poverty, abuse, or violence, his SNS and PSNS are hyper-stimulated. In these scenarios, safety is elusive, and the smart vagus neural pathways get little chance to implant and develop. Accordingly, children from unsafe early-childhood environments develop a nervous system that is dominated by the stress response system, which is highly associated with increased rates of both morbidity and mortality.

*

Acceptance is another quality of relationships that is critical to health and well-being, and the capacity to feel accepted by others is greatly influenced by permanent, supportive relationships in childhood. Being accepted, or feeling like you belong, registers in the dorsal anterior cingulate cortex (dACC) of the brain, a thin strip of tissue deep in the frontal lobe. Recent research by Eisenberger and Lieberman at UCLA has highlighted the role the dACC plays in our pain system. In a novel social experiment, these researchers studied "Why It Hurts to Be Left Out."[8] Subjects entered the social science lab believing they were simply playing computer ball toss with two other people. The goal was for the individual being studied to continually toss a virtual ball between their character and two other similar characters on the screen. Over the course of the game,

8. Naomi I. Eisenberger and Matthew D. Lieberman, "Why Rejection Hurts: A Common Neural Alarm System for Physical and Social Pain," *Trends in Cognitive Science* 8, no. 7 (2004): 294–300.

the person being studied is left out of the ball toss game in order to study the effects of exclusion and rejection. While the "pain" of being left out of a ball toss experiment would seem minimal—especially when compared to the pain in real life of being left out of a relationship or social group because of your skin color, financial status, sexual orientation, or any other characteristic that differentiates you from others—it was far from zero. The researchers were actually surprised to learn that most people who participated in the study reported feeling quite badly about being "left out." Subjects reported that it actually "hurt." What's more, when the researchers looked at the brain activity of the subjects, they found that those who reported experiencing pain at being left out had a measurable increase in the activity of their dACC.

This led Eisenberger and Lieberman to perform further research on the dACC, and their work produced a very interesting result. The dACC has long been known to be the area of the brain activated by the distress of physical pain. The implications for this shared function of the dACC are immense. Their resulting model, which they named "social pain overlap theory," proposes that to human beings—arguably the most social of all animals—being left out of the group was so perilous to survival that the neurological alarm system that alerts the individual to the danger of exclusion is shared neurologically with the alarm system for the danger of physical pain. Essentially, they propose, *being left out of a social grouping is so hazardous to humans that we developed so as to devote the same neurological pathway to exclusion as we do to pain.*

This leads me to the parallel consideration I have raised in previous sections of this paper: What happens to the dACC of children who do not experience nurturing permanency in childhood—children who grow up unassured of their next meal, or the safety of their own bed, or the competency of their adult caretakers? We know that such children develop highly reactive pain pathways. In contrast, children who are lovingly nurtured, held, comforted, and made to feel safe in their early lives develop a nervous system where the sights, smells, sounds, and touch from contact with nurturing adults are neuronally wired to an internal sensation of pleasure and calm. But when a child's world is chaotic, unsafe, or neglectful (even when that was not the intent of the adults immediately around him), the sight, smells, sounds, and touch associated with contact with adults can trigger the development of an overactive alarm system. In turn, the stresses and protective distancing produced by their overactive alarm system can leave these children at risk of seeking alternative methods of comforting and soothing themselves. Drugs, alcohol, and other self-destructive behaviors are all too often used to numb the chronic pain of the isolation these children experienced from having to distance themselves from the incompetent adults in their lives.

*

"Resonance," the *R* in the CARE program, refers to the ability humans have to "know" other individuals intuitively, which includes not just reading another person's actions but also intuiting their sensations and emotions. Humans do this through their "mirror neuron system." Mirror neurons were discovered in the late nineties by researchers in Italy who were studying a small, specific area of the brain in rhesus macaques that allowed the monkeys to reach out and grasp something in their environment. The research involved placing an electrode directly into the F5 neural area of the monkeys' brains. The researchers noticed that as a monkey was watching a person reach for an object, the F5 area of the monkey's brain activated as the monkey moved its arm in a mimicking manner. This was shocking and confusing data. Initially, the researchers assumed that the monkey was moving its arm to "mimic" the behavior of the person he was observing. However, with more controlled observations, they determined that this was not mimicking in the sense of children playing "mirror" but instead involved mirror neurons that *internally mimic* the actions of the other. This chance finding opened up a whole new understanding of how people read and know each other.

Two decades have now passed since this initial discovery, and the field of mirror neuron studies has shown repeatedly that humans know and understand others through internally mimicking their behaviors. Recent research describes how this basic process works, and how humans use previously developed neural networks to create an internal template of perceived actions of the other. For example, if I watch you reach out to shake another person's hand, the prefrontal cortex—the area in my brain that would plan and execute the action of reaching out and shaking hands—is activated. Additionally, since I have had the experience of shaking hands in the past, the area in my somatosensory cortex that registers sensations like touch, pain, friction, and so on will be activated, so not only do I have an internal feeling of my hand shaking (when all I am doing is watching you shake another person's hand), but I also can sense the particular feel of what it is like to touch another person's skin. Finally, assuming the handshake I am witnessing is a pleasant greeting, a signal will be sent through my insula to my visceral system, creating a feeling of warmth. In the end, these pathways are activated immediately and spontaneously, and they provide me with an embodied sense of what you are experiencing when you shake someone else's hand, even though I have not moved a muscle.[9]

This neurological ability to intuitively read another person's actions, sensations, and emotions is developed in the earliest of childhood relationships, so once again, having permanent, safe, nurturing caretakers to develop healthy pathways for

9. Christian Keysers, *The Empathic Brain* (Social Brain Press, 2011).

connection and resonance is critical. Without nurturing, safe adults, the neurological "wiring" will be haphazard and chaotic. Take, for example, the case of a child whose home life is disrupted because of domestic violence. Assume the battered wife is able to flee the home with her child and to create a new life that is less violent but still stressful and chaotic. Let's also assume that the child witnessed his mother being grabbed and battered by her partner, who was angry and out of control. For the child in this hypothetical case, his mother's admirable efforts on his behalf may be too late to negate what was neurologically implanted: when later in life the child sees someone reach toward him—even innocently—this might activate the child's old trauma pathway. So, even if the person now reaching out to the child is well intentioned, the resulting initial reaction of the child may be determined by the child's neurological experience that reaching out ends in violence. It would, accordingly, not be unusual for such a child to pull away, or to become suddenly frightened or frozen.

Another aspect of accurately reading another involves "mentalizing." Mentalizing involves matching your internal resonance with past learned experiences. And the role of permanence and parental consistency is critically important for a child to successfully develop the ability to match his internal feelings with an accurate account of what is happening in the external world. I often describe an example from my own parenting that hammered home this point to me. When my twins were six years old, I was driving them to school along a familiar route close to home. As we approached an intersection, another van turned left and hit us head-on. The crash was violent and the damage extensive: both vans were totaled. The airbags deployed, sending fumes and gases throughout the car. The engine was spitting water from the radiator, and almost immediately the rescue vehicles came upon us with a cacophony of sirens and alarming sounds. In an effort to comfort my children, who must have had adrenaline rushing through their bodies, I jumped into the back seat and looked into their worried faces and said simply, "Everything is okay." While I certainly now understand my need then to reassure them that everything would be okay, what I did was actually danger-ous. Why? Because, if I did it over and over again, I would be labeling an emergency that they were feeling in their bodies as "okay." Fortunately, my wise son looked right back at me and said, "Everything is *not* okay, this is a bad accident!" Even at the time, this remark allowed me to backtrack and say what I really felt—how scary this was—and then to check to see if they were *indeed* okay. It was a valuable lesson for me. Though I still have the instinct to gloss over painful events or to rename them in the most positive light, I also now understand that my job as a parent was to name all emotions as accurately as I could so that the body sensations my children were experiencing could be used to accurately read what other people were experiencing.

Again, we see that children who do not have nurturing adult permanence, or who are worried about where their next meal will come from, or whether their bed or home is safe, lead lives that are filled with stress that often is neither accurately named nor addressed. How could one expect otherwise: the adults around such children are often equally overwhelmed. Operating out of *their* fear centers, such parents find it very difficult to tune in and resonate with the children in their care, and—from our point of view—part of the harm that results lies in the fact that the children's brains are still in the critical developmental process I have been talking about.

The effects of the Trump administration's controversial efforts to curb illegal immigration by separating children from their parents when they cross the Mexican–United States border can be understood by the application of the above dis-cussion on "mentalizing." The political strategy—described as a "deterrent" by high-ranking Trump administration officials—is based on the assumption that other parents will abort their illegal efforts to cross the border if they understand that their children will be taken from them. The political response of critics of Trump's policy was that the policy is shortsighted and un-empathic and fails to take into account that this family-based immigration involves people fleeing their homelands because of danger in their own countries. The administration's response to this criticism was to employ rhetoric that was designed to characterize illegal immigrants as the "other," as "less valuable than" natural-born Americans or those who were vetted and legally allowed entrance into the country.

For our analysis of mentalizing, what is interesting to glean from this example is the danger in this approach *for those who do the "distancing"* (a different danger than those suffering the effects of the forced separations). This occurs because the ideological tool of making someone else an "other" leads to a decrease in the functioning of the mirror neuron system in he who does the distancing. In other words, he who would distance others for ideological purposes does so by unnaturally elevating the part of his brain responsible for abstract reasoning (the ideological content) over the part of the brain evolution has designed to employ in the process of understanding other people (the mirror neuron system). On a sociopolitical level, this has the effect of promulgating biases from one generation to the next; but what is interesting for the purposes of this paper is that we can see how, on a neural level, this puts the brain at war with itself.

*

The fourth characteristic of a healthy relationship is the feeling of energy or zest produced when interacting with safe others. As I described earlier in the Positive Relational Moment

(PRM) exercise, taking a moment to remember a PRM will have an effect leading to an increase in energy. Energy (the E in the CARE program) refers to the degree to which the dopamine reward pathways remain connected to healthy, secure relationships. With the evolution of mammals, the dopamine reward system developed so that activities that were in the best interest of the individual or species triggered the release of dopamine in the dopamine reward system. This dopamine acts as a "carrot" to reward behaviors like eating nutritious food, drinking water, procreative activities (sex), and healthy, safe contact with others. In other words, evolution has made us all Pavlov's dogs: we are provided a shot of dopamine filling us with energy, motivation, and good feelings when we undertake the basic activities that promote survival of the individual, and thereby the survival of the species.

Louis Cozolino, a psychologist who researches the neuroscience of relationships, has gone so far as to say that the healing process would require cessation of substitute stimulation of the dopamine reward system and reattachment of it to healthy relationships.[10] Unfortunately, this is easier said than done in today's Western cultures with their emphasis on separation and individuation as the ultimate goals of healthy human development. Depending on the degree to which achieving independence from others is emphasized by adult caregivers as a sign of strength and the goal of "growing up," a child will internalize the message that needing close relationships with others makes him weak or needy, rather than healthy and an integrated member of a community.

Once again, we can trace the pathology of the absence of permanent, nurturing family relationships during childhood—this time on the energy element of the CARE analytical model. Children raised in impermanent, chaotic settings never

---

10. Louis Cozolino, *The Neuroscience of Human Relationships: Attachment and the Developing Social Brain* (New York: W.W. Norton, 2006).

"learn" to connect the dopamine reward system to healthy relationships, and it is precisely in early-childhood relationships—with all their cuddling, cooing, nursing, and feeding—that the initial dopamine relationship pathways must be built. Once the window for the creation of these pathways closes—once a child is "built" without its neural pathways biochemically connecting stimulation of its dopamine reward system to nurturing relationships, the neuronally malformed child will, as an adult, seek out other means of stimulating its dopamine reward system. Why this dopamine transfer? Because the need to stimulate the dopamine reward system is an absolute: doing so is inextricably linked to how humans summon up the energy and motivation they require to face the tasks of everyday life. Accordingly, children raised in impermanent, chaotic settings never "learn" to link the production of naturally produced dopamine with stimulation by nurturing and stable relationships. These children, by default, grow up to be considerably more likely than the general population to turn to other sources to stimulate their dopamine reward system. Mix this with the fact that we live in a culture where artificial chemical and nonchemical sources of substitute stimulation are omnipresent, and the results are perfectly predictable. Drugs, alcohol, online gaming, pornography, manic shopping—all these are just a sampling of the repetitive behaviors that can be used to stimulate the disengaged dopamine reward system for a quick fix. And take note of the negative spiral that this substitution can entail: many of these addictive, repetitive behaviors end up pulling those who employ them ever further away from healthy relationships, which in turn leads to ever-higher employment of substitute stimulation. So, it's not so much the chemistry of the drugs and alcohol that leads to ever-greater substance abuse by disconnected individuals—it's more fundamentally the biochemistry of the individuals themselves.

*

I have tried in this brief paper to sketch out a shorthand description of how the CARE model understands the development
and functioning of the neural pathways for connection. For
each of the four elements of the model, I have also attempted to
outline just how important nurturing, safe, early relationships
are to the developing child. In the end, the lesson learned from
the neuroscience of connection is that healthy, stable human
connection—most especially during childhood—is absolutely
essential to the neurological development and thus to the long-
term neurological health and mental well-being of individuals and thereby to the communities they make up. Given the
robustness of the literature in this sphere, it is heartening to
learn that social welfare organizations are out to develop programs for families and children structured precisely around
the importance of permanency.

The Home for Little Wanderers is one of these organizations. For over two hundred years, The Home has been operating in the greater Boston area to help support children and
families in need—in just this way. These services are described
as "wraparound," which, for the children The Home serves, is
the next best thing to the stable home environment the children never had. The Home operates on the underlying principle that keeping children and families together and at home
is social work's top priority—if the child's home is safe. To
accomplish this, The Home provides multiple types of support programs to failing parents who have been identified by
the Massachusetts Department of Children and Families. The
entirely admirable goal of The Home, and its sister institutions,
is to keep children in their homes where they can develop their
neural pathways for connection in a safe environment, with
family permanence and stability as the primary goal of the
social work. Each year, The Home serves over seven thousand

individuals with programmatic support that ranges from parental skills building to clinical therapy to facilitating education. And when it must—and only when it must—The Home provides substitute residential care programs for children whose homes cannot be made safe. In essence, The Home and its sister agencies serve as society's safety net for children in need, so that they can grow and develop their neural pathways for connection. Ultimately, the work of these agencies significantly increases a child's chances of developing into an adult who is built with the need for connection with others, and who is equipped to provide nurturing and permanency as a parent.

III

Thoughts on Children and Loneliness

JACQUELINE OLDS, MD

Loneliness in children is a topic that fascinated me even as a child. Perhaps this was because my family moved many times during my childhood. During these years, we lived in four different cities—Cambridge, Massachusetts; Montreal; Los Angeles; and Ann Arbor—which meant that I was often quite alone, and quite lonely, being the new kid at school who had no friends. There were many, many lonely times before I finally learned to overcome my inhibitions and take the initiative to try and make friends. And above and beyond my own inhibitions, my parents were intense academics who focused only on their work, their work-based friends, and their kids. Period. When I think about it, they didn't set much of an example at all about how to strike out and make friends—this was something I had to figure out for myself. So, given my personal history of childhood loneliness, it is a fascinating endeavor for me to try to think through why children today might be even lonelier than they were in the past.

In this paper I want to address four main points. First, why children need social interaction; second, what the difference is between what a child learns from its relationships with its parents/caretakers as opposed to what a child learns from its relationships with its peers; third, what it is in our current era that inhibits relationships between children and leads to more childhood loneliness than characterized earlier times; and fourth, what we psychiatrists and other mental health professionals can do clinically when we are faced with a child who tells us that they are lonely.

First, let's talk about what a child receives from their earliest days from a loving parent or an effective caretaker. Here is a quote from Alain de Botton, a Swiss philosopher, found in his essay, "On Soothing":

> It's the middle of the night, let's imagine we've been on the Earth for about three months. A lot is still very unclear. We are profoundly helpless, barely able to move our own head, and utterly at the mercy of others . . . Hugely powerful needs pass through us at regular intervals and we have no way of making sense of them to ourselves, let alone of communicating them reliably to others . . . In a rising panic when we feel uncomfortable, we start to scream out in the darkness. Nothing happens. We pause to recover our breath—and then scream even louder. Our lungs strain with the effort. Still nothing, and the darkness and loneliness grow ever-more threatening. Now true desperation sets in; this feels like the end of everything good and true. We scream as if

to ward off death. At last, just when it seems we could not go any further, the door opens. A warm orange light is turned on. It is a familiar face. They smile at us, say the name they often use around us, pick us up and put us against their shoulder. We can hear a familiar heart beating next to ours and a warm hand caressing the top of our head. They gently move us to and fro, and sing a tender sweet song. Our sobs start to abate, we pull a weak smile; it feels like the vicious demons and merciless goblins have been sent packing, and life could be bearable after all.[11]

Now the reason these words from de Botton are so moving is that, even though we might not be able to remember our own childhood, we each know full well whether this sort of soothing came easily and naturally to our own parents. In looking back, of course, some of us recognize that we had parents who felt so beleaguered (or perhaps were inadequately soothed themselves as children) that they never developed either the skill of self-soothing or the capacity to sooth others—including us. As adults, of course, we can fully understand that to a child whose parents never developed the skill of soothing, the world must seem a frightening and unwelcoming place. And, of course, for a child to develop the capacity to self-soothe—and later the skills to soothe their own children—it is hugely advantageous to have been soothed by a loving parent or caretaker. Arguably, one explanation of why today we have so many more lonely children who seem positively imprisoned in their loneliness is that there are many factors in modern society that have interrupted the cycles of soothing that have been such

---

11. Alain de Botton, "On Soothing," *The Book of Life*, https://www .theschooloflife.com/thebookoflife/on-soothing/.

an integral part of child raising throughout human history. Without appropriate parental soothing and the learned ability to self-soothe, growing up can be quite a lonely proposition, because life—perhaps in general, but certainly in our era—is filled with so many everyday blows to the ego that can cause such great emotional pain.

This brings me to one of the central ideas of my model: in the process of growing from childhood to adulthood, one necessarily experiences the ever-lessening physical presence of caretakers ready to protect, nurture, and instruct. This gradual physical fading away of one's parents, necessary though it is, has the consequence of producing many moments of loneliness for the child being progressively left on their own—even in the best of circumstances. When you add in the many different struggles and happenstances with their peers that find their way into any child's life, there are always moments—and hours and weeks—where the child experiences the pain of finding himself alone. Ilg and Ames, in a famous book on child behavior from birth to age ten,[12] commented on the fact that there are, typically, *entire years* in a child's early development that are tinged with melancholy—as if a child is, in some senses, in mourning over the gradual fading away of its parents, notwithstanding that this is inherent in the process of growing up. A year later, when Ames reapproached the same topic and split the analysis into multiple books about separate age ranges, she gave one book the title: *Your Seven-Year-Old: Life in a Minor Key*.[13] The hypothesis was that there are times in a child's development when the child is going to feel somewhat "out of whack." Ames gives as an example the circumstance in which a child finds himself stressed out, unable "to feel at

---

12. Frances L. Ilg and Louise Bates Ames, *The Gesell Institute's Child Behavior: From Birth to Ten* (New York: Harper Collins, 1985).
13. Louise Bates Ames and Carol Chase, *Your Seven-Year-Old: Life in a Minor Key* (New York: Delacourte Press, 1985).

home in [his] own skin," because his cognitive development has outstripped his emotional development.

So, what I am arguing is that there is—*necessarily*—a considerable amount of loneliness inherent in the very process of growing up—for all children. But, of course, above and beyond this endemic loneliness, there are children who experience an overdetermination of their lonesomeness because of the adverse circumstances of their upbringing. And these children will be at risk over their lifetime to experience still more loneliness as adults. The goal of this paper is to explain why this is so.

*

One inescapable aspect of passing from childhood to adulthood is moving on from being completely self-centered—as infants necessarily are during their "completely cared-for phase." As a child matures and begins to achieve perspective on their own life experiences as compared to those of others, they learn step by step to put themselves in others' shoes. This process often takes until young adulthood to achieve, and it is dependent, to a significant extent, on having peers to compare notes with. But to successfully compare and contrast one's own experience with that of others, one needs to interact and connect with others—and, particularly, with peers above and beyond one's siblings. In the absence of information gleaned from peers raised by other parents, very little perspective can be achieved, and socialization and interaction skills are not learned—to a child's serious detriment. For such children, each personal feeling is experienced in isolation without the sense of comfort that comes from learning that others have experienced that feeling as well. The experience of having little or no perspective as to whether what one feels in reaction to life's experiences is normal or abnormal, permanent or passing, threatening or benign—causes a child to feel lonely and uncertain, and even unsafe.

Many years ago, when I was the psychiatrist in charge of a children's unit at McLean Hospital—a psychiatric hospital located in Belmont, Massachusetts—we provided residential treatment for a goodly number of very isolated children who were extreme cases of children raised without significant contact with other non-sibling children. It was typical for them to very quickly lose perspective. And some of them were so incapacitated by their early-childhood experiences—by the absence of successful interaction with non-family peers—that even though they might later spend years in elementary school around other children, it was too late: when they got upset, for example, they would still wail like an infant.

Allow me to outline one extreme case that illustrates how interpersonal connection deficiencies—loneliness—in a child's upbringing can interact with other mental problems to make clinical treatment significantly more difficult to achieve. The case involved an incredibly cute little seven-year-old boy—who we'll call "Jimmy"—who came onto our unit at McLean because he had been preoccupied with death and feelings that his body was falling apart. His school's guidance counselor thought coming to an inpatient unit might shed light on why he was in such a depressed state. As we got to know him, we came to understand that both his parents, who were highly educated, had been suicidal when he was about four. They had a history of marital difficulties and had fought frequently since that time, including in front of their children. The parents didn't socialize much and worked a great deal. On top of this, they had had to move four times since Jimmy's birth because of the father's work. Jimmy had two siblings who were also somewhat emotionally shaky, and the parents had arranged for therapy for Jimmy and one of his siblings. Even after clinical counseling, Jimmy had remained unable to make any non-sibling friends and strongly disliked attending school. We learned from Jimmy's teachers that he was often irritable in school and that he lost his temper very quickly and easily. He was, in my opinion, a child without allies: his parents and siblings were unavailable to him because of their own significant issues, and he was also without friends or any other supportive, nurturing connections outside of his home.

A typical therapeutic play session with this child involved my making a scribble drawing and asking Jimmy what he saw in it. Jimmy saw one of my scribbles first as a lady with clouds above her in the sky. Then he told me to draw a picture of clouds all touching each other. Then he told me to make rain and lightning coming out of them. Soon, he wanted to make burning bombs coming out of the sky and people underneath the sky bleeding. He then covered the whole page with red and black scribbling, obscuring all of the picture. I ventured to say to him that people in the picture must have been "very scared" and asked him if he ever felt that way. He responded, "It's just a picture." But later in the session, there was progress: Jimmy admitted that he often got into fights at school. And he added that sometimes during these angry outbursts, his head felt "like it might explode."

You don't have to be a child psychiatrist to see that Jimmy was seriously depressed. He was by nature, however, open to listening. Progressively, the boy became more aware that his repetitive fighting at school was the product of his not having made any friends there. He began to see that his isolation added considerably to his anxiety and depression—and the more we spoke together, the more aware of this he became. Bit by bit, session by session, he became more able to admit to himself and express how lonely he felt at having no one to listen to him talk about how his parents didn't get along and that they argued so much. Additionally, Jimmy became progressively more able to see and talk to me about how seeing his parents mired in their marital conflict and personal states of depression meant that he couldn't see anything welcoming about the world of grown-ups.

While I hope my professional efforts—and those of other staff in the unit—were helpful, a great deal of the credit for Jimmy's ensuing improvement has to go to the other children. Their contribution was a perfect example of the critical importance of non-sibling interaction among children. Many of the children in our inpatient unit themselves had significant family troubles, like Jimmy—an absence of supportive, nurturing, stable adults. But, somehow, these troubled children realized that they had among themselves a potent and available resource—each other. Tired of being isolated and feeling so lonely, these children began making sound friendships with each other, and the smiles and mutual support for one another began snowballing on a daily basis. We encouraged it, of course, but it principally happened by some spontaneous recognition by the children themselves that in increasing the level of acceptance of and connection with each other, they were each seeing more sunshine in life, day by day. Jimmy, along with the others, began making friends for the first time in his life, and as the days went by, more and more smiles broke out across his cute face. After two months of being coached and supervised by us, and two months of rewarding connections made with the other children, Jimmy began to understand and value what it felt like to be embedded in a web of supportive connections. Before long, Jimmy was able to go to a residential school where he adjusted pretty well, all things considered—and he almost immediately exhibited his newly acquired skill of daring to strike out to make new and supportive friendships with the other children in his classroom.

*

Special problems arise for a child who is being raised by a parent or parents who themselves suffer from loneliness. Such children have less perspective, less know-how, when it comes to their trying to make their own friends.[14] Sometimes, such children may hang back like their parents do, or exhibit desperation in their efforts—and hence fail to connect. They are out to avoid the loneliness they see plaguing their parents' lives, but wanting to connect and having the skills to do so are not the same thing. On top of this, efforts to form friendships by such children are not always encouraged by their parents, because far too many of these isolated adults overly rely on their children for company. We repeatedly find in child psychiatry, for example, that school refusal is all too often a function of a needy, lonely parent who cannot "spare" the child's company for six hours per day. There are also isolated, lonely parents who interfere with their children's learning how to reach out and make new friends—because they are concerned about their children's capacity to keep family secrets. This can prove especially problematic for these children, because self-revelation and "telling one's secrets" are often the currency of how children make and keep friends. So, if a child is forbidden to tell secrets, they may have trouble with both making and keeping connections, and hence with practicing the methods by which one does so. For these and other similar reasons, it was not rare for us to work with children whose loneliness was very intimately related to fulfilling their parents' needs.

Not surprisingly, in such cases, if you can make inroads into the isolation and loneliness of the parents or caretakers, you could at times initiate a ripple effect that lessened the likelihood that the parents or caretakers would pass on to their children their inability to successfully make connections. A captivating piece of research on just this issue has been

---

14. Jacqueline Olds and Richard S. Schwartz, *The Lonely American: Drifting Apart in the Twenty-first Century* (Boston: Beacon Press, 2009).

contributed to the literature by a husband-wife team named Philip and Carolyn Cowan.[15] They found that when they started a parents' group for expectant parents at six months into their pregnancies, and continued the group until the newly born children were three months old, these six-month-long group sessions had a statistically significant positive effect on both the marriages and the children's development—and that the effect lasted throughout the several years in which longitudinal data was gathered. There was something about the parents having a chance to compare notes with other new parents that had the effect of allowing them to be kinder to each other (significantly fewer divorces than in the control group by three years post pregnancy), and they were more nurturing to their children (multiple measures of this are cited in the Cowans' book). The study seemed to show that if therapeutic group sessions made inroads into the sense of isolation and loneliness that new parents or caretakers often experience after the birth of a child, the sessions could cause a ripple effect that lessens the subsequent likelihood of isolation or loneliness among the children. What I love about this study is that it demonstrates an intervention we mental health professionals can make that improves the connective capacities of both parents and their children—and it's one that is not at all expensive or difficult to arrange. I would think that with a minimum of initiating effort, mental health professionals could each launch a number of seasoned parents into serving as leaders of this type of group for brand-new parents—and thus have an outsized, snowball effect for their efforts.

We need to also acknowledge (and somehow learn how to deal with) the fact that we live in an era when even the best of parents and caretakers sometimes isolate their children from

---

15. Carolyn P. Cowan and Philip A. Cowan, *When Partners Become Parents: The Big Life Change for Couples* (Mahwah, NJ: Lawrence Erlbaum Associated, 2000).

playmates for sociological reasons. In today's world, there is a general sense of "danger," and parents are quite reasonably reluctant to allow their children to walk around in their neighborhoods and ring a friend's doorbell to see if another child can "come out and play." Even in prosperous neighborhoods, parents are ever-more protective of children in this way, and ever-more likely to feel that they must arrange playdates to ensure that their children are safe and secure. Many parents in our era feel that even an arranged playdate must include adult supervision, and with an ever-higher percentage of mothers working full time, these supervised playtimes are more and more difficult to arrange. The response of many parents entrapped in this dilemma is to arrange a series of scheduled lessons, tutoring sessions, and the like for after-school hours— for the learning opportunities involved, to be sure, but also so that the parents can feel assured that their children are safe. And when you add this to what was discussed earlier—that all too often in this age of "loneliness," parents may be reluctant to give up their children's company when the child is serving as one of the adult's "best friends"—you have the perfect recipe for producing yet more loneliness in the generation to come.

On the bright side of the ledger, let's not forget that children are very resilient by nature, and that children of the past have survived far worse circumstances than the loneliness that characterizes our era. Children are resourceful by nature: many who spend a great deal of time alone employ the adaptive mechanism of developing imaginary friends. In doing so, children are exhibiting a capacity to keep *themselves* good company. Note that when children develop imaginary friends because they are lonely, we do not consider this psychiatrically problematic the way we might with an adult. On the contrary, child psychiatrists generally feel reassured that this creative venture exhibits a desire for connection that indicates a healthy valuation of connection that foreshadows future friendships and successful interpersonal linkages.

We also live in an era of new technology that allows a child to connect with their peers by text or on the Internet, and the percentage of cell phone activity that is made up by adolescents chatting and texting with one another throughout the day must be astounding. So even if the children of our era, compared with those of the past, spend a relatively large amount of time alone, they are often electronically linked with one another— or with the mass media. Through these new technologies, as well as through their school interactions with others, children work to learn and hone the skills of connecting with others to form the linkages and friendships that keep loneliness at bay.

I want to take just a moment to review the rare but interesting circumstance in which parents bring their otherwise psychiatrically normal child to a child psychiatrist and report that the child is failing to make friends—or failing to make enough friends. In some—but certainly not all—such cases, the doctor and the parents can work to reengineer the child's life so that the situational framework helps rather than hinders the child's chances of successfully connecting with other children.

More often, however, the psychiatric condition of the children we see who have trouble making friends is not known to us when we first encounter these children, and there may well be a complicated reason for their plight. Suppose that we hear about a child who seems lonely to his parents, neighbors, teachers, and relatives. How do we evaluate whether the child's isolation emanates from a personality problem—meaning that there is something in the child's personality that the child is unaware of that pushes people away—or whether the child's problem is generated by parents or caretakers who have failed at the job of encouraging and helping their child to learn how to make friends and successfully enter into rewarding social relationships?

If possible in such a case, we of course interview not only the parent or parents but also other collateral adult caretakers such as the child's teachers, trying to learn what they have noticed about the child from its earliest days. If we learn that the child was serious and noncommunicative from infancy, we can attribute the connection and attachment issues to the child's personality and temperament—especially if the parents seem normally sociable.

But a very different type of case is presented when parents report a particular precipitating incident that, by their observation, caused the child to shut down their communications and/or to withdraw from the process of connecting with others. In such a case, a treating mental health professional desperately needs to gather a detailed history in order to learn the specifics of what took place that made that child give up on interacting with and relating to others—especially his peers—and to instead decide to "keep their own counsel." Typical stressors leading to this type of withdrawal might include the death of a beloved relative or a childhood illness that was both serious and traumatizing. Other cases have been triggered by a change in family fortune that left everyone in the family humiliated to the point where they broke off from frequenting their old friends and acquaintances due to the embarrassment of what had become public. And, sadly, we have seen many cases where some sort of abusive situation has rendered the child ashamed and depressed—and has triggered the child's withdrawal.

Practically speaking, how do child psychiatrists and other mental health professionals who treat withdrawn children go about this critically important detective work? While, of course, we begin with taking an extensive history from parents, siblings, and teachers, only the child can inform us of a good deal of what we need to learn. The difficulty with this, of course, above and beyond a young child's language limitations, is that we typically cannot address the problem "head-on" with the child. Most children in therapeutic settings feel so embarrassed about feeling lonely and not having friends—or about not having the capacity and skill set to make friends—that they are in complete denial. They often lie about their actual degree of isolation, and sometimes they refuse altogether to talk about the topic. So, rather than taking a frontal approach, often the most productive clinical tactic is the tried-and-true method of "working in displacement," or play therapy, in which we use make-believe characters to tell a story that has some elements of the child's conflict.[16] This technique allows a clinician to make interventions in the story that give a new message to the child that subtly counters their worldview that not trusting others is their safest option. To give just one example, there is a technique in child play therapy called the "mutual storytelling technique." In it, the therapist can interview the child on a "pretend" radio program and ask them to tell you about themselves as a celebrity whom they admire. Then they can subsequently interview the therapist, playing the radio announcer while the therapist acts out the role of the "pretend" character. This simple technique provides many an opportunity to slip in indirect advice about both the importance of connecting with others and how to successfully go about it.

I would like to report more deeply on this technique, since it has worked successfully for me with many children who were psychiatrically normal but who were overtly reluctant to reach out and connect with other children to form friendships. It wasn't difficult to convince these young patients to make up a personality for a pretend "radio interview," and typically they would expound on their plans to live on their own throughout their life. When I, as the radio show interviewer, would ask why they would want to do that, the most common response was because including others just leads to their hurting you

16. Kevin J. O'Connor, Charles E. Schaefer, and Lisa D. Braverman, eds., *Handbook of Play Therapy* (New York: John Wiley, 1983).

and taking your things. These children were essentially artic-ulating the position: "Who needs friends? Better to keep your stuff in a secure place away from others so you can enjoy what you have." Gradually, in this set of interviews, I would begin to introduce the question, "Isn't having toys and other good things more fun if there's someone to share them with and play with?" (Practice note for clinicians reading this paper: this approach works far better if the therapist is actually *fun* for the child to play with. So be fun!) If the child persists in their certainty that other children—and adults—are greedy, mean, lying cheats, I often ask: "So in your world, everyone's just awful and you can't trust them at all. But because of my job, I've known lots of other people's worlds who have told me that the people around them weren't all so bad! I wonder why everyone in your world is so greedy and mean?" The impact of this approach—when it works—is that the therapist can com-municate to the child that the world they know is very limited; as they grow and set out on their own lives, they will be able to find and create very different interpersonal circumstances than those they experience in their particular home and school setting. The goal, of course, is to encourage the child to start to question their own assumptions in light of their learning from a new grown-up whose experiences in life have led them to be far less pessimistic about the value of striking out to make—and keep—friendships with others.

So, let's assume a therapist has made real progress with a child and is ready to begin advising the parents and/or care-takers about the reintegration of the child into their milieu—whether on coming out of an inpatient setting or after the conclusion of extensive outpatient clinical sessions. The ques-tion becomes: How to advise the parents and/or caretakers so as to maximize the chances that the transition will be success-ful? To begin with, clinicians need to remember that children need a lot of help in changing their behavior patterns, and if

the parental patterns and home circumstances that contributed to the child's inabilities to successfully connect with others have not changed, one cannot expect the child to move
on from their previous tendency to elect isolation. How can a
clinician go about getting these children to assert their newly
learned connective skills? To do so, frankly, the clinician often
needs to turn practical and real-worldly. For example, if the
therapist thinks the child is ready to try playdates with other
children, but the parent is still working so much that he or
she cannot afford the time to supervise the playdate—or otherwise arrange for playdates—then clearly the transition will
never happen. Mundane as it may seem, in such a circumstance it is time for the clinician to help the parent figure out
some real-world, practical solutions. Or take another set of
circumstances that are all too common: if the neighborhood
to which the child is returning is still too dangerous, and the
other children likely to be befriended are so delinquent that no
sensible parent would want to arrange a playdate with them,
then again, it's time to turn practical.

In other words, our work as child therapists is often a
delicate balance of suggestion, knowing the resources, and
figuring out some practical ways in which the parents and/or
caretakers can change the child's environment so as to allow
the child to exhibit and practice their newly acquired hunger
for and capacity to connect successfully with others. This may,
for example, involve investigating a child's particular neighborhood with the parent and thinking strategically together about
how to achieve affordable transportation if the child cannot
play safely in their own neighborhood. Sometimes helping the
parent investigate and make use of appropriate after-school
programs has proven a good and affordable way to help the
child become accustomed to other children's free play in a
semi-structured environment. By the way, a clinician's word to
the after-school program supervisor about a particular child

needing some help with socializing skills has often brought out creative efforts by daycare teachers.

Some children, of course, are so angry and embittered by the isolation and loneliness they have suffered, that routes to successful therapy are far harder to find. At McLean Hospital, we often saw children who were furious about their lack of friends, and who were brimming over with rage about feeling shortchanged or deprived of one of life's great pleasures. At times, the anger of such children made them fantasize about how to gain fame by a huge act of rage—and several referenced a fantasy about effectuating a school shooting. This, they thought and explained, would make others take notice of their sadness and deprivation. Frankly, it was frightening to hear these violent fantasies because they demonstrated that for the same reasons adolescents are so subject to fads, they are subject to the contagiousness of the school shootings they see displayed and discussed in vivid detail on television. It was not rare for me to hear these angry fantasies from ostracized, lonely adolescents who fantasized about achieving fame by doing something awful. When I look back at the angriest adolescent patients on our unit, or when I study the published accounts of teenagers who engage in fantasies or actual violent actions against others, I see that it is often because they felt left out or rejected by peers. Such children often express a fantasy about "getting even" with the children who didn't include them, but they also fantasize about taking out their revenge on children in general—and especially those who experience the joy of connection and inclusion.

So, while we are on this topic, it behooves us to ask whether or not mental health professionals who specialize in treating children could indeed do something of scale to prevent some of these mass-killing catastrophes. After every school shooting, some argue for gun control, while others argue for psychological profiling to identify potentially violent adolescents before they strike. Others, of course, take the position that we need to proceed along both paths simultaneously. As for the path that concerns us here, we might indeed be able to up our game to engage in preventative psychiatry. With the right resources, we would, to some extent, be able to locate these "left out" children and work with school and community authorities and organizations to find ways to include them. The goal would be to break the cycle of loneliness that extends from these boys to the destroyed lives and inestimable loneliness of those who lose children in school shootings. The key question, of course, is whether we live in a society that is prepared to provide the resources that would be required for such an undertaking to succeed at scale.

One successful example of tackling this issue can be found on many of the nation's college campuses where the administrations have realized the importance of making available for their students a plethora of choruses, plays, and sports activities at all different levels, as well as a panoply of clubs specializing in almost every conceivable interest. I cannot imagine a better investment than encouraging the same wealth of opportunities for "left out" kids to join with others of like interest in high schools and junior high schools. This, I would argue, is an entirely more realistic means of reducing school violence than relying on mental health and educational professionals to somehow identify, report, isolate, disarm, and cure those few angry, isolated, lonely adolescents who will actually turn violent.

I want to include just a few thoughts about sexual identity and loneliness in our contemporary adolescent culture. In many ways, concerns about sexuality in today's society begin at an ever-younger age. Part of this, of course, is a function of the younger age at which contemporary girls experience menses as compared with earlier generations. Obviously, the media and Internet pornography play their role as well. But what I want to point to for the topic of this paper is that in our era, young people who are only eleven or twelve years of age feel the need to declare the nature of their sexuality because they are expected by their peers to join with other kids in groups to "support each other." Some have wondered if this is driving young people to declare their sexual preferences much too early, especially if their motivation for doing so is to stave off loneliness by joining with others who are similarly questioning and confused. What I am arguing here is that for children who feel like misfits or outsiders, joining a victim's group creates a very different type of connection than joining a club or interest group or sports team. This is because the psychological experience of joining others in defense—in this case of some given form of sexuality—does not confer on the adolescent adherents the same opportunities to advance their skills in connecting with others. Bonding between children formed in a defensive posture is delimiting by its nature: the lesson is to connect only to those who are like you. In contrast, bonding between children pursuing a common interest is expansive by nature: the lesson is to befriend anyone who exhibits an overlapping interest. The former reduces the population with whom a child can connect, while the latter expands the universe of potential new friends.

*

I want to make two final points in closing. First, I cannot exaggerate the amount of practice with face-to-face interactions it takes children over many, many years to learn how to take turns sharing attention, how to become a good sport, and how to tolerate the bruises of everyday life. Interacting with others throughout preschool, elementary school, junior high school, and high school—as well as the noneducational activities provided in neighborhoods and by voluntary interest groups—provides the training ground on which children learn how to reach out and make and maintain friendships. All those bruises on the knees and elbows of young children have their emotional equivalents in the bruises to their psyches that adolescents necessarily suffer in the process of learning how to interact and connect with others.

Given the critical importance of learning connection skills by practicing them during years and years of childhood inter-actions, it becomes obvious that we do a serious disservice to our children by overly protecting them from roaming the neighborhood or by scheduling their entire after-school day so that they have no time left for neighborhood friendships and casual non-sibling interactions. The twenty-minute lunch/playground period at school simply does not provide enough time for the development of interaction patterns that children need. If we wonder why so many more students are lonely at college or why the suicide rate at college continues to climb, we might need to look back at high school, middle school, and even elementary school to learn when and why these college students failed to develop their connection skills. Given the extent in our era to which we prevent children from having adequate opportunities to develop their connective skills in unstructured after-school play time, we can predict that they will have trouble all their lives forming and keeping friendships.

The final point I want to make is that I think children also need some "boring time" to master the art of solitude and to learn how to make use of their own inner resources. Sometimes each of us finds ourselves alone; the challenge, of course, is to become skillful at being alone without feeling lonely. The psychologist Mihaly Csikszentmihalyi studied the science of contentment and found that the more *flow* activi-ties a person has, the more he or she will be content in adult life.[17] He defines "flow" as an activity that is so enjoyable that

---

17. Mihaly Csikszentmihalyi, *Flow: The Psychology of Optimal Experience* (New York: Harper Collins, 1991).

you forget the passage of time and feel like you could do it for-ever. When we are children, we often have activities that we could do forever, be they basketball, reading, drawing, arts and crafts, or—in the modern era—video games. These activities to children are so enjoyable that they hate being interrupted—even by the parent who calls the child to come have supper. But often in adulthood, we forget how essential these activ-ities are to our sense of self. Or how they stood us in good stead when our friends weren't around. Or how they motivate us to use free time to reengage in our favorite flow activities, as opposed to succumbing to the use of a substance when we find ourselves alone. In adulthood, to the extent we can each find our grown-up version of these flow activities, we develop the inner resources to get through difficult times and, more specifically, the capacity to be alone without feeling lonely.

*

My research confirms that we are experiencing a wave of increasing loneliness in children—entirely in keeping with recent studies documenting the same significant uptick in chronic loneliness for adults. And I am talking about chronic loneliness—not the garden-variety childhood loneliness we all knew from time to time as we grew progressively more independent from our parents. I'm referencing children whose psychological well-being is threatened by the deeply isolated and desperately lonely childhoods they are experi-encing—children such as those I've mentioned and referenced in case summaries throughout this paper. These children are spending as much or more total time with their parents as did earlier cohorts over the past decades: absentee parents are not the problem. Instead, the principal factor generating contemporary childhood chronic loneliness is the simple fact that today's children are not spending enough time interacting with other non-sibling children. What can look to adults like senseless play and repetitive sporting events are far more than a pastime for children: it is in these interactions with each other that they learn the skills of connecting and bonding with others, finding new friends, and avoiding bullies—all important skills. When circumstances disallow such free play, we are, in effect, producing the next generation of chronically lonely adults. My hope, of course, is that the pendulum will swing back to allowing children to have more neighborhood time with other children for free-flowing friendships. We need to make our neighborhoods safer—for sure, but we also need to not exaggerate the degree of danger that our neighborhoods currently present—because our children need to get back outside, and start knocking on each other's doors, repeating the famous phrase, "Can Johnny come out and play?"

IV

An Adult Psychiatrist Looks at Loneliness in Childhood

RICHARD S. SCHWARTZ, MD

Do you see a hint of apology in my title? My wife, Jacqueline Olds, is the child psychiatrist in the family, not me. But since we usually tag along with each other when we talk about loneliness, here I am. My hope is that as an adult psychiatrist who's thought a lot about loneliness, I bring a new perspective in looking at the research on children and loneliness for the first time, and I might end up with something innovative to contribute to the discussion.

Here's the first thing I discovered when I tried to immerse myself in recent research on children and loneliness: there isn't very much of it. Over the last couple of decades, there's been an explosion of research about loneliness in adults, but very little about children. It's not that nobody cares about lonely children. Put "lonely child" into a Google search, and your heart will melt in a sea of poignant images. There's just not much formal research to tell us more than we already know.

By contrast, we've learned some remarkable things about loneliness in adults. And what we've learned has finally grabbed people's attention—headline-generating attention, like this one from the *Boston Globe*: "'Loneliness kills': Former Surgeon General Sounds Alarm on Emotional Well-Being."[18] The most important thing we've learned is that social connection matters more to our health, well-being, and longevity than—well, just about anything. In the words of a consensus statement from an international conference on attachment and bonding, "Positive social relationships are second only to genetics in predicting health and longevity in humans."[19] We've learned that our connections to others affect us at the most basic level of genetic expression—where genes are turned on and off, mostly genes that control our immune system.[20] We've learned that the subjective experience of loneliness and the objective fact of social isolation each shorten our lives independently; each makes a difference.[21] And we've learned that, since World War II, we as a country have become both lonelier and less connected.[22]

What part of this applies to childhood? How much of today's "epidemic of loneliness" has its roots in childhood? And picking up a point from Jacqueline Olds, who also

---

18. Felice J. Freyer, *Boston Globe* (January 16, 2018).
19. 2003 Dahlem Workshop on Attachment and Bonding.
20. Steve W. Cole, Louise C. Hawkley, Jessica M. Arevalo et al., "Social Regulation of Gene Expression in Human Leukocytes," *Genome Biology* 8, no. 9 (2007). In a groundbreaking study, DNA microarray analysis identified 209 genes that were differentially expressed in circulating white cells from lonely versus not lonely individuals.
21. Julianne Holt-Lunstad, Timothy B. Smith, Mark Baker et al., *Perspectives on Psychological Science* (2015).
22. AARP, "Loneliness Among Older Adults: A National Survey of Adults 45+," (September 2010). In 2010, 40 percent of adults over forty-five said they are lonely, compared to 20 percent in the 1980s.

presented a paper at the symposium "Loneliness and the Power of Permanency"—the symposium that generated this edited book—what is changing these days that affects the development (or lack of development) of children's friendship skills?

I stumbled upon a quote from the children's book editor Ursula Nordstrom where she references her qualifications. "Well, I am a former child and I haven't forgotten a thing." My memory's not *that* good, but the first part certainly applies to me. When I think back on my own struggles with childhood loneliness, I think about the fact that I grew up in a three-generation household: two parents, two grandparents, and me—the only child. So I was more embedded in an old-fashioned extended family than most kids around me were. This meant I was essentially never alone at home.

But I was a shy child, which was probably due as much to my inborn temperament as it was to a lack of practice in contact making. About 15 percent of us are born shy. It's an important factor in loneliness, but it's not a rigid destiny. There are many more shy children than shy adults, which means we can learn to be less shy.

So here I was, surrounded by so many adults, living in a Manhattan neighborhood where I couldn't just step out my front door and be swept up by a gang of kids. I was one of the children Jacqueline Olds describes who learned the skills of connecting with grown-ups long before I learned how to connect with other children. So, as a child, I was both lonely and not lonely at the same time. Interestingly, in my psychiatric work, I've met many patients who describe the exact opposite experience—they experienced an aching distance from their family members from which they were regularly rescued by close connections with their friends. This split—the way loneliness inside and outside the family can be independent of each other—makes childhood loneliness much more complicated to study and understand.

The same split can be there for adults, but it hurts less. I've been talking a lot recently about loneliness and friendship in middle-aged men. In a study Jacqueline Olds and I did years ago,[23] we stumbled upon an interesting fact. We were looking at marriage in couples with young children. Every single man we interviewed expressed a desire to be more involved with his children than his father had been with him. Each man described having a demanding job, with long hours at work and often more work to take home. Something had to give. What gave for most of the men was friendship. They still "had" friends—they just never saw each other or talked much with one another. They felt bad about it, but they reported they didn't feel lonely. They were immersed in relationships at home and at work. The loneliness would come later, with empty nests and retirement.

In childhood, having rewarding connections in one of these two arenas doesn't seem to buffer loneliness in the other. And, as Jacqueline Olds has written, the skills a child needs to overcome loneliness in relation to adults and the skills a child needs to successfully connect with and make friends with other children are not at all the same skills. Part of what sets up loneliness in adulthood is not having had the opportunity to learn the skills of making and keeping friends as a child. And the absence of such skills is all the more likely to have serious consequences for those children for whom connection does not come naturally. Shy children, for example, are at significantly greater risk. So are children who grow up in neighborhoods that don't give them an adequate opportunity to step out in the street and find themselves surrounded by other kids. Almost ironically, this opportunity for children to learn their connection skills from neighborhood play is often missing these days

23. Jacqueline Olds, Richard S. Schwartz, Susan V. Eisen, R. William Betcher et al., "Part-Time Employment and Marital Well-Being: A Hypothesis and Pilot Study," *Family Therapy* (1993).

in both neighborhoods of high privilege and neighborhoods of hardship.

What are the mental health consequences of mixed states of loneliness and connection, like being lonely at school and well connected at home? It's a fascinating question that I can't answer, but there are a few hints from studies of adults. The largest and most up-to-date meta-analysis of loneliness and health was published by a group from Brigham Young University in 2015.[24] It was based on data from seventy independent prospective studies, with more than 3 million participants, each followed for an average of seven years. The increased likelihood of death was 26 percent for reported loneliness, 29 percent for social isolation, and 32 percent for living alone. The magnitude of the physical health effects on morbidity and mortality is right up there with smoking. They're greater than the risks from obesity or lack of physical activity. What's particularly fascinating to me is that there is essentially no difference in effect between objective and subjective measures of social isolation. Being alone and feeling lonely are equally bad for you, even though you can be lonely without being isolated and isolated without being lonely. If that conclusion applies to children, it means that children who feel lonely despite lots of apparent social contact in school or at home are still at risk. Most lonely children are not really alone, but that might not be good enough to protect their health.

While I can't take it all the way back to childhood from published research, I can tell you that the impact of social connection on our health starts early, at least as early as adolescence. Drawing on four nationally representative longitudinal samples, one group looked at the *prospective* association between measures of social connection and objective

24. Julianne Holt-Lunstad, Timothy B. Smith, Mark Baker et al., "Loneliness and Social Isolation as Risk Factors for Mortality: A Meta-Analytic Review," *Perspectives on Psychological Science* (2015).

measures of physical health, things like C-reactive protein, systolic and diastolic blood pressure, waist circumference, and BMI—markers that precede getting sick.[25] What they found was that social integration is related to better physiological functioning and lower risks of physical disorders across life stages, in a dose-response fashion. What that means is that the more socially integrated you are, the healthier your biomarkers look. And it begins at least as early as adolescence, because we know that adolescent social connections predict health risks in young adults. In other words, the physiologic processes that lead to poorer health in adults are already at work in socially disconnected adolescents. I could locate no data on how this plays out in younger children. The study referenced above didn't include them, presumably on the assumption that wider social networks don't impact health until adolescence. I don't know if that's true.

There was one phase of life with *no* significant association between social connections and any of the biomarkers. It was midlife—approximately thirty-five to fifty-five years of age. I already mentioned what's special about that time. During those middle years, most people are so naturally embedded in multiple social networks, through work, community, and family, that there's a kind of automatic protection against social isolation, which is what the study looked at. But that doesn't address the concern we still need to have about loneliness. It also doesn't tell us about people who, despite the odds, are still socially isolated in midlife (or childhood).

The truth is, it's hard to know how to count social contacts these days, especially among young people. Social media have created an entirely new category of connection. A marketing survey in 2016 found that three-quarters of American

---

25. Yang Claire Yang, Courtney Boen, Karen Gerken et al., "Social Relationships and Physiological Determinants of Longevity Across the Human Life Span," *Proceedings of the National Academy of Sciences* (2016).

teenagers (ages twelve to seventeen) owned and used a smartphone.[26] For fourteen- to eighteen-year-olds, the number was 87 percent. It's certainly even higher today. We have a generation of teenagers who are making that crucial adolescent shift in primary connections from family to peers while immersed in ways of relating to others that never existed before. Does that make them more lonely or less lonely?

The most ominous warning comes from the social psychologist Jean Twenge. She found a steady and striking rise in unhappiness among American teenagers that began in 2010—the year that the number of Americans who owned smartphones passed 50 percent.[27] Most of the increased unhappiness is in girls. It's not clear what that means. But with a database of around five hundred thousand teens, Twenge found a "dose-response" correlation between unhappiness and screen time. The more screen time, the more unhappiness, and the more suicide-related behavior. But there's more. Some activities were associated with *less* unhappiness. All of them were "non-screen" activities, including "print media" (I think we used to call that "reading") and doing homework. (Tell that to your kids.) There are lots of questions about the study: it's just a correlation, the data on depression is soft, the data on screen time is from retrospective reports, and we don't know what the teens were actually doing on their screens. But the study's findings do get your attention. They strongly suggest that connecting through screens is different from non-screen connections, raising the question of *why* connecting through social media does not protect us from unhappiness the way old-fashioned, pre–social media does. What might account for the difference?

---

26. eMarketer, "Devices Owned by US Internet Users, by Age" (February 2016).
27. Jean M. Twenge, Thomas E. Joiner, Megan L. Rogers et al., "Increases in Depressive Symptoms, Suicide-related Outcomes, and Suicide Rates Among US Adolescents after 2010 and Links to Increased New Media Screen Time," *Clinical Psychological Science* (2018).

One possibility is that those old-fashioned social connections are not just social, they're physical. The orbitofrontal cortex, which plays an important role in social judgment, receives sensory input from all five senses and our internal organs.[28] Face-to-face contact gives us so much more data to work with as we learn to deal with others, to get along with them, to feel connected to them. Teens who spend a lot of time on social media are trying to learn how to navigate a complex social world with a much narrower bandwidth of data, even if that data is bombarding them all the time.

That narrow bandwidth is particularly important for children who are lonely because they haven't learned the skills of friendship, or because they are the "odd ducks" who come across as just a little different and never quite fit in. The social world of screens makes it especially hard for them to learn the skills of friendship. On the other hand, it also gives them a way to connect with others that they may find more manageable— precisely because it is more constricted and less spontaneous.

A 2010 study from Australia found that lonely children and adolescents spent more time in online communication than did normally socialized children; they used the Internet to meet new people to compensate for their weaker social skills.[29] It looked like it worked for them. Lonely children and adolescents communicated more frequently about personal and intimate topics online than the children who were not lonely. That sounds like a good thing, but it leads to an important unanswered question: Is online connection a bridge to the skills and confidence that will let these lonely children eventually have

---

28. Jennifer S. Beer, Oliver P. John, Donatella Scabini et al., "Orbitofrontal Cortex and Social Behavior: Integrating Self-Monitoring and Emotional-Cognitive Interactions," *Journal of Cognitive Neuroscience* (2006).
29. Luigi Bonetti, Marilyn A. Campbell, and Linda Gilmore, "The Relationship of Loneliness and Social Anxiety with Children's and Adolescents' Online Communication," *Cyberpsychology, Behavior and Social Networking* (2010).

satisfying offline relationships, or does it end there, where it began, with connections at a safe distance?

"Will" is a patient of mine who reports that he was one of those odd-duck kids—a touch of autism, and a congenital problem with eye movements that was undiagnosed until he was twelve. It made him terrible at sports. The teasing and bullying began in first grade and didn't stop until two years before college when he changed schools. Much of the time, he was completely friendless and frankly afraid of encountering anyone his own age. He was also depressed. For him, the online world was a godsend, a place to have safely constrained connections with others through gaming and programming projects. There's a study underway to see if Facebook can be used intentionally to improve the lives of lonely patients with major mental illness by providing social support that is simply not forthcoming to them in the "real" world. The online world worked for Will—up to a point—but it didn't teach him the skills he needed for offline friendships. He was still terrified of putting himself at any risk for rejection. He never reached out to anyone in a way that opened up the possibility of friendship. He spoke in a tone of constant superiority and condescension that pushed most people away. At first, it put me off too. (His single most positive response to my many insightful comments was, "There, you're not entirely wrong.") When he came to see me, my first task was to treat his depression, but the bigger challenge for him was to learn how to connect with others in ways that he could never learn on his computer. Will is a work in progress. A couple of years into it, he reports that he has some friends and feels less alone, and also that he's approaching his distance from others as a problem that he can now slowly resolve.

I don't want to sell social media short. We may yet learn how to use them wisely. Early studies of the Internet found that spending more time online meant spending less time with real people. A few years later, new research indicated that that was no longer true. Even in Twenge's data, more screen time does not correlate with spending less time with people face-to-face. I talked about the "thinness of social media" compared to the sensory richness of face-to-face contact, but long ago, human beings learned how to make another "thin" mode of communication extraordinarily rich. If I pull out a volume of the collected letters of—just about anyone—it makes my own face-to-face communications sound pretty pathetic. Perhaps with any new mode of communication, it takes a while to figure it out.

But since the symposium that in turn led to this edited book began with one of J. W. Freiberg's remarkable stories called "The Loneliest Boy," I want to end with one more story from my practice.

Michael was in his late adolescence in a city in the Midwest, when he began to experience symptoms of schizophrenia. His parents found excellent treatment for him, but it wasn't helping much. His treatment team recommended a move to McLean Hospital for long-term inpatient treatment. That's a phrase that dates the story: that doesn't happen often today. I was a young psychiatrist in charge of an inpatient unit. Michael arrived a little before Christmas, and it didn't take long for me to learn that he was an extraordinarily talented pianist. I remember the warm feelings on Christmas Eve when Michael played the piano and patients and staff gathered around, first singing carols and then listening to an impromptu concert. A few weeks later, Michael escaped watchful eyes and locked doors. By the next day, he was dead by suicide.

His parents came back East to meet with me. They told me that if anyone wanted to do something in Michael's memory, they should give a donation to the music school back home that was the one place he felt he belonged. *A place he felt he belonged!* The referral letter to our hospital had said the transfer made sense partly because there was no one Michael felt connected to back home. But there *was* a community where Michael felt he belonged—his doctors just didn't know about it. So, in seeking better treatment for him, he was abruptly uncoupled from where he would have felt more connected and, presumably, safer.

How much did that disconnection matter in his suicide? I'll never know, but a few weeks later, another patient at McLean also died by suicide. She happened to come from the same city in the Midwest. I did a small study on the effect of hospitalization far from home on suicide rates. It turned out that it did matter, but only for patients under thirty. Without my realizing it, Michael's death awakened me to the importance of social connections to our very survival. It also opened my eyes to the systemic neglect of its importance in mental health treatment—an importance that may still be there for an individual even when the connections look weak or deeply damaged. That was true for J. W. Freiberg's "loneliest boy." In a small way, I hope this edited book growing out of the April 2018 symposium on loneliness and children can help us all keep our eyes on that ball.

V

Growing Up Lonely

*Disconnection and Misconnection
in the Lives of Our Children*

J. W. FREIBERG, PHD, JD

Introduction

In my recent book, *Four Seasons of Loneliness: A Lawyer's Case Stories*, I proposed that "loneliness" is not an emotion, but a sensation. Loneliness, I suggested, operates precisely like its sister sensations, thirst and hunger: it is a perception of an absence, of something missing. Thirst warns us of inadequate hydration, hunger signals inadequate sustenance, and loneliness alerts us of inadequate connections. The title *Four Seasons of Loneliness* was simply a reference to the fact that we are subject to feeling inadequately connected, or "lonely," in all the phases—or "seasons"—of our lives.

There are important consequences to conceiving of loneliness as a sensation and not an emotion. This is because sensations are primal: we share them with the substantial entirety of the animal kingdom. In contrast, emotions are quintessentially human overlays. Parched and famished animals sense their thirst and hunger, and they follow determined patterns to seek water and food. In addition, most animals, and essentially all mammals, seek not only water and nourishment but also, to differing degrees, the company of their like-kind for security, breeding, and the raising of young. Of course, a nonhuman mammal cannot conceive of *why* it seeks companionship—it isn't equipped to "feel lonely" in the way we do. Instead, it is simply and directly driven by its neural pathways to rejoin its breed, or to locate a mate, or to raise its young—all without the emotional overlay we humans add on top of and also in response to our sensations.

So, why is this important? Because if our perception of our disconnectedness is indeed a sensation, that means that the feeling of loneliness is controlled and processed, as are our other sensations (except for audial input), by the parietal lobe of our brain, *over which our conscious mind has no control whatsoever.* Emotions, in contrast, are effectuated by the limbic system, which is located in the temporal lobe, particularly the amygdala. This distinction is critical: whereas we can make conscious input into temporal lobe functioning, quite the opposite is the case with parietal lobe, or "old brain," functions. This is why you can talk yourself out of being angry (an emotion) but you can't talk yourself out of being hungry or thirsty—or lonely (three of the sensations). And if that's true, and if Dr. Amy Banks is correct in her paper in this volume that human children who grow up afflicted by disconnection or misconnection with their parents actually fail to develop the neural pathways needed for a fully functioning capacity to connect effectively with others, then it is hardly surprising that chronically lonely children are far more likely than the general population to become depressed, chronically lonely adults, and to suffer from appallingly higher rates of morbidity and mortality.

A Word on My Methodology

My somewhat unique approach to studying loneliness in the lives of our children comes from my having had two quite divergent trainings. I taught courses in social psychology, social theory, and the sociology of law until a curious set of circumstances led to my attending law school. Three years later, I began my law career at one of Boston's premier firms, planning to practice trial law in Boston's United States District Court and appellate law in the United States Court of Appeals for the First Circuit. But, as it turned out, legal practice in Boston involves a great deal of case referral—attorneys are actually encouraged by rules of the state's supreme court to refer new cases that are outside their area of specialization to another attorney with appropriate experience. Being the only attorney in Boston who had taught social psychology, I was soon typecast as Boston's "psych lawyer." The Home for Little Wanderers—the venerable agency that sponsored the symposium from which this book arose—was the first to approach me, and in 1985, I became The Home's general counsel, a position I was to hold until my retirement from the active practice of law some thirty years later. Almost immediately, the Italian Home for Children, Child and Family Services, Stevens Childrens Home, and a number of other smaller agencies offered me the same honor, and they were soon joined by over half a dozen adoption agencies and scores of private clinical practices of psychiatrists, psychologists, and social workers.

While each of these corporate entities required routine legal work—a lease for new office space, review of a proposed contract, employment and insurance issues, negotiation and litigation of disputes with third parties, and so on—their individual mental health professionals needed case consultations on a regular basis. Over time, this consultation element of my work grew exponentially as clinicians found themselves confronted with a constantly increasing number of regulations and rapidly changing jurisprudence—with which they were required to comply. So, an ever-growing component of my responsibilities as general counsel to these agencies consisted of fielding an ever-increasing flow of case-specific legal consultations. These calls came in on almost a daily basis and involved my hearing a detailed description of a patient's overall circumstances, and then responding to whatever particular legal question had presented itself. This meant that for thirty years, I heard and took detailed notes on more than a thousand social-psychological fact patterns from which arose the clinicians' legal questions, and these case-specific notes form the database from which I write today about children and families.

My methodology is simple and straightforward: I begin with my case notes from these consultations—for purposes of this particular paper, only those involving children—and try to identify which cases shine the brightest light on the topic at hand. Then, I simply allow the case stories to speak for themselves. This is what I did in *Four Seasons of Loneliness: A Lawyer's Case Stories*, and it seemed to work passingly well. I have subsequently employed the same methodology—if that term is even merited—for a book that will be published shortly after this edited work under the title *Surrounded by Others and Yet So Alone: A Lawyer's Case Stories*.

Four Seasons of Loneliness was a study of the chronic loneliness suffered by those who are profoundly isolated and alone in the world, devoid of the interpersonal connections each of us need to thrive and be safe. In contrast, *Surrounded by Others and Yet So Alone* is a study of the chronic loneliness suffered by some among us who subsist in a network of unrewarding relationships that fail to provide the positive effects enjoyed by others who, in contrast, form and are nurtured by gratifying connections. This second type of lonely person lives among others—parents, siblings, a spouse, children, friends, partners, colleagues, neighbors—whatever—but their connections are of a deficient and unsatisfying nature: they fail to provide the safety, the soothing, and the nurturing warmth that soundly connected persons derive from their relationships. In a word, their connections are defective and constitute what I call "misconnections."

The Challenge Children Face in Our Era of Misconnection

Seth Doe, "the loneliest boy," whom you met in the first story in this collection, is the poster child of *disconnection*. When I last saw him, he was permanently and definitively cut off from everyone in his family, and at eighteen he headed out into this cold, hard world utterly cut off from every single person he had ever known. While we'll come back and take a close look at his case in the final section of this paper, the first four children you will meet were threatened with chronic loneliness not because they were *disconnected* from their parents but because they were *misconnected* to them.

When I reread my child-centered law case notes in preparation for writing this paper, I found that just under a fourth of these children presented as chronically lonely—often alongside a host of other issues. Roughly half of these lonely-children cases involved significant *disconnection* issues—no great surprise, since many of these children had been institutionalized after being removed from their grossly dysfunctional families by the Department of Social Services.[30] But the other half of these lonely children still lived at home with their parents and siblings, and they were often enmeshed in multigenerational families and vibrant neighborhoods. So the loneliness that half of these lonely children suffered was not a function of their *disconnection* from the adults in their lives, but instead was a product of their *misconnection* with their parents and other significant persons with whom they lived.

The more I studied my case notes involving children whose misconnection with their parents was the source of their loneliness, the more I perceived that these cases fell out into five types, or what I call "modes of misconnection." That is, there seemed to be five principal patterns of misconnection that reappeared over and again in multiple cases. They are as follows:

- **Obstructed Connections:** When something blocks connectivity
- **One-Way Connections:** When the connectivity runs in only one direction
- **Fraudulent Connections:** When the connection is flawed by misrepresentation
- **Tenuous Connections:** When the connection is uncertain, tentative, or provisional
- **Dangerous Connections:** When the connection is fraught with torment and peril

So, for each of these modes of misconnection, I have chosen one representative law case that seems to best illustrate how loneliness can enter and degrade the lives of misconnected

---

30. The name "Department of Social Services" was subsequently changed to "The Department of Children and Families," but I employ the name of the era in which I practiced.

children. Each of the five discussions below begins with a brief presentation of the selected case story—although space considerations force me to provide you with only a portion of each tale. Following each such story, you'll find a brief discussion of what the story has to tell us about how challenging, and sometimes how damaging, misconnection can be in the lives of children. So, be forewarned, my reader: for each mode of misconnection, I will be asking you to shift gears as the study moves from case story to analytical discussion.

A Note on Privilege and Confidentiality

Those who have read early drafts of these stories have inquired, almost to a person, if they are fact or fiction. These stories come from the files of actual law cases on which I worked, and they contain a myriad of details about the lives of clients whom I counseled and represented. That being said, limits imposed by privilege and confidentiality requirements oblige me to modify identifying specifics of the cases from which these stories are drawn. I do this by changing names, altering identifying details, shifting locations, integrating elements from related law cases, and modifying some components of the actual cases I litigated, negotiated, and consulted on. But rest assured: the lessons about misconnection and loneliness that speak out from these stories come from very real law cases indeed.

Obstructed Connections: Billy's Case

At ten years of age, Billy Denver was the youngest client who ever retained my services. He was also one of the cutest: at just about three feet tall, Billy's straight black hair and impish smile made him look like a miniature Paul McCartney—except for his eyes, where he had the Beatle beat hands down: Billy's eyes were precisely the color of robins' eggs.

Billy's case came my way thanks to Evan Newsom, MD, one of Boston's most renowned pediatricians. Newsom's practice was centered at Boston Children's Hospital, where years earlier, he had started one of the nation's first child-abuse counseling and treatment programs. The program had pioneered new techniques in discovering abuse and neglect in young— even preverbal—children, and had developed bold new innovations as to how to clinically examine and treat young victims of molestation and family dysfunction. I had originally come to know Newsom through my work as general counsel to The Home for Little Wanderers when I consulted with him on a case involving a sexually abused child. In the years that followed, I asked him to serve as an expert witness in numerous court trials in which such matters were at play.

It was a bright and crisp spring day when Doctor Newsom called, one of those magically clear days that help you forget the seemingly endless Boston winter that you'd somehow survived. Newsom explained that he had a ten-year-old patient in his unit who suffered from lymphoma—a dangerous cancer that attacks the lymph nodes and then all too often spreads from there. The boy was the only child of educated, high-achieving parents: his father was a super-busy hedge fund/investment person of some sort, who, in Newsom's opinion, didn't visit often enough, and his mother was the twice-elected mayor of the tony suburban town where the family lived. On the surface, the family relationships seemed normal enough, but according to Newsom—something was wrong, something was missing.

When I asked for more details, Newsom told me—in his airline-pilot-calm voice—"There's a grayness, there's a sadness to the boy that I can't explain. And I'm almost certain it's not an emotional reaction to his medical condition. It's more than that." He explained that he couldn't discern any hints of emotional abuse or neglect—and no one was better at picking up these signs than Newsom and his team. And, of course, if he had found even a *suggestion* of abuse or neglect, as a "mandated reporter" he would have been required by law to alert the Massachusetts Department of Social Services. But there wasn't a hint of either. There was only what Newsom described as a "persistent cloud over the boy." He told me that he had used every trick in his bag to get the boy to talk to him about the issues that were worrying him, but all to no avail.

"All I got out of him," Newsom continued, "was that there is a 'legal issue' involved—whatever the hell he might mean by that. That's why I thought of you, Terry. Help me figure this one out, would you? I've *no* idea what's going on here: all I know is that this little guy is just a month or two shy of some tough-ass chemo, and he needs these clouds to part so he can help us fight this thing." He went silent, waiting for my reply.

So, you tell me: What could I possibly say but, "Sure. No problem."

*

Just a week later, I pulled into the Children's Hospital parking lot, on my way to meet with Newsom and his patient. And then I saw Billy. I don't know what it is that can attract and connect one person to another so immediately, but I fell under Billy's spell the moment I met him. He was a cute-looking little kid, for sure, but looking back I can see that it was more likely the sense of calm and resolve he radiated: rare traits for a boy of ten.

Initially, Billy showed complete disinterest in me until Newsom mentioned that I was a lawyer who did a good deal of legal work that had to do with children. At this, the boy lit up like a switch had been thrown, sat up more against his pillows, and announced in as serious a tone of voice as his littleness could muster, "Well, that's just great, because I need to retain the services of an attorney—*now*." As you well might imagine, Newsom and I burst out laughing, and I think what first *really* touched me about this child was that he joined right in.

Newsom soon excused himself, leaving the two of us alone. And here, in just a few words, is what Billy told me. He was the child of a successful family where everything material was readily supplied. He described some of the material advantages he enjoyed, precisely in order to contrast them with his description of the one thing—beyond good health—that was missing in his young life: *unremitting parental love.* According to Billy, his dad had neither the time, nor much discernable interest, in fathering—as opposed to just *being* a father. But, he added, lots of his friends had hyper-busy fathers, so this wasn't his principal complaint. The real problem lay with his mother, who, again using Billy's words, "doesn't seem to be able to love me very much." I remember physically wincing when he said this, and I'll never forget the clarification he followed up with: "No, I'm not saying this right . . . I know she does love me . . ." He took his time to find his next words. "But she does love the way a flashlight shines light when its batteries are just about dead. It's just a glow: it doesn't help you see your way in the dark."

I was completely taken aback by his remark, and stood there in silence, stunned.

"That's why I need a lawyer or a private eye or something," he added. "I need to learn why that is."

Billy looked over at me with his robin-egg eyes and radiant smile, waiting for a response. You can imagine what it felt like to have to disappoint him, but I had no choice: because he was a minor, the law didn't allow him to retain counsel. And even if I could be his attorney, I went on to explain, there is no law that requires parents to be effective in how they love their children. Of course, there *are* laws that require parents to keep their children safe, fed, clothed, housed, in school, medically attended to, and so on—but there is no statute compelling effective loving.

Even as I spoke, I could see the deflating effect my words were having on Billy, and . . . that was just not where this needed to head. So, quite unprofessionally I might add, I invited Billy to tell me more, to give me all the details he thought were important—and then we'd see together what, if anything, could be done.

*

Billy spoke from his heart for the next quarter hour, and by the time he'd finished, everything had changed. I learned three things from him that day: first, that he was absolutely determined to find out precisely *why* his parents gave him so little emotionally; second, that he was resolute about fixing whatever was broken; and third, that he desperately needed an ally to proceed.

And, mind you, he wasn't looking for free legal services. On the contrary, he insisted that his savings at home were just shy of seventy-nine dollars, and that he was willing to invest that "entire amount" in my legal fees. I didn't dare smile at this offer; he meant it with dead seriousness.

I had an idea, I told Billy. Given that I was general counsel to a child welfare agency called The Home for Little Wanderers, if he met with one of The Home's social workers, and if the social worker called me for a legal consult, then perhaps I could formally represent The Home while working on his case. I couldn't promise anything, but at least it was a possibility. I was preparing to reword what I'd said to make certain it was all clear when Billy dispossessed me of any such concerns: "Clever strategy." Ten-year-olds don't talk like that. Who was this little kid?

Later that afternoon, I reached The Home's clinical director and told her about my meeting with Billy. She came through in spades, and arranged for a clinical social worker to visit him at the hospital the following day to see what the story was. Two days later, when her notes had been transcribed, the clinician gave me a call.

Sure enough, the little guy had fully convinced her that there was a significant—if subtle—problem in his relationship with his parents. Moreover, she was deeply impressed with the boy's determination to get to the bottom of why he felt so emotionally starved. Reading from her clinical notes, she described Billy as "charming," "insightful," and "hungry to connect better with his parents." But she also described him as "somewhat saddened" and "emotionally undernourished." Like Dr. Newsom, she also had concluded that Billy's sadness was not a function of his medical issues, serious though they were. The wording she used in her summary struck me, so I quote her from my case notes: "It sounds like the parents 'love' him in some formal sense, but that neither of them seems capable of making him *feel* loved." Better yet, she also reported that her clinical director had told her that I was welcome to intervene as counsel to The Home. We agreed that I would see if I could convince the family to seek family counseling to work on their connection issues.

I wish I were poet enough to put into words the excitement in Billy's voice when I spoke to him by phone the following day. He seemed in no way surprised to learn that he had convinced the social worker of the worthiness of his cause, nor did he sound perplexed when I told him that although I couldn't formally serve as his attorney, I could watch out for his interests in serving as The Home's counsel. More concretely, we agreed, I would contact his parents to see if they would meet with me. I cautioned him, however, that the misconnection with his parents that he was describing did not amount to "neglect" in the legal sense of the term—so I would have little or no leverage to use if his parents didn't volunteer to speak with me. But I would try. Billy's response is in my telephone notes: "Perfect. They'll listen to you, I'm sure of it. I'm a great little kid, except for being so sick. There's no reason why they shouldn't love me better. They just need to learn how."

I remember thinking how significant it was that this little tyke said "better" and not "more." And I thought it was remarkable that he didn't for a second internalize the incomplete love that trickled down to him. He seemed to have total confidence that he was entirely lovable and that the deficiencies in the parental love that came his way sourced from something wrong with *them*, not from something wrong with him. I was to learn that he was entirely correct.

*

When I finished that phone call with Billy, I was on a mission: I now took it as a personal challenge to get at least one of Billy's parents up and working. This little guy was going into chemotherapy, for God's sake, and, if I'd understood Dr. Newsom correctly, he might subsequently need radiation therapy as well. While it was true that his father made weekly visits to his bedside and that his mother visited on nearly a daily basis, their physical presence was somehow failing to transmit the emotional connection that Billy craved. The boy couldn't *feel* their love for some reason. He couldn't tap into it; he couldn't fall asleep reassured by it. There was child-parent connection here, but it was defective to the point where Billy sensed it as misconnection.

*

For no particular reason, I started with the father. Billy had given me both of his parents' work phone numbers, so it was easy to reach his father's secretary. Reaching the father, however, was quite another matter. Understandably, his administrative secretary demanded details as to just who I was and just what I wanted. And it wasn't that easy to formulate a convincing answer, given that my client was The Home, and especially because the agency's involvement in the case was so entirely collateral. In any case, I failed to make any progress whatsoever and was just about to get cut off—so that left only one option: "Tell him that if he doesn't call me back about his son, my client may well file a Chapter 119, Section 51A report of child neglect against him with the Department of Social Services." For some reason, the statute numbers did the trick: it was a toothless threat, but it got me an appointment on the spot.

*

Billy's father, I was to learn, was all about money. He was a principal in a private equity company that, I was informed, was a stone-cold player in the game of buying up well-run local companies, loading them with debt to pay the company's fees up front, and then cannibalizing the company by selling off its intellectual property, market share, and physical assets. Then it was time to close the company, lay off its employees, and move on. My source told me that these hard-edged strategies had put many, many people out of work and changed the face of a number of neighborhoods.

When I walked into this gentleman's office, he never came out from behind his desk to shake my hand; in fact, his very first words were "I only have fifteen minutes for you. Big meeting at ten o'clock. Sit down. And you should know that the only reason I'm giving you even this much time is because my lawyer said I should. He said you could cost me a truckload of wasted time if you hassled us by filing some kind of report about our parenting." I was stunned into silence, hoping that his own words would echo in his mind. Could the next business deal really be more important to him than the well-being of his only child?

Yep. Turned out it was. I tried to explain to him that Billy was emotionally starving at a time when he desperately needed full connection with his parents, but the father gave me exactly the same blank stare I gave to a math-professor friend of mine who once, over lunch, tried to explain to me his work on "differential equations." It became immediately clear: William Denver wasn't going to get close to being open to what I was saying to him. I thought perhaps he was trying—he seemed pensive and inward looking. I remained still as a cat until he found what he wanted to say: "Look, Counselor, I love my son, of course. The problem isn't me. It's my wife: since she's gotten off into the mayor thing, she's as busy as I am. Busier. I keep telling her, it's her responsibility to make time for the kid."

I was greatly tempted to call it a day; after all, the quarter hour was almost up. But I didn't dare lose the opportunity to probe about the mother, even if I went—God forbid—overtime. "So, let's talk about your wife, then. Billy said that he knows she loves him but that he can't *feel* her love. Those were his exact words. What do you think he meant by that?"

The venture capitalist in his two-thousand-dollar suit went stone silent again. He looked down at his right hand, which was skillfully twirling a pencil around his thumb and then re-catching it, over and over again. I had touched a nerve— or rather, Billy had. His voice even choked up a bit when he finally responded. "She's like that with me too. Billy's right. I don't know what it is in her that makes her love so lukewarm. I used to want to shake her, to wake up the emotional part of her, almost." He paused again, still spinning the pencil around his thumb; and then, after ten or fifteen seconds of silence, the doors into William Denver's heart closed as he came back to the present. He looked up and concluded our meeting: "Go see her, Counselor. Go figure her out." He paused a moment and then announced that we were, "unfortunately," overtime.

*

Just a few days later, Dianne Denver sat down in a chair across from my desk. Clearly the source of Billy's charms, her face was framed in silky black hair that she had pulled back in a ponytail. You immediately sensed Denver's self-confidence in the way she held herself, and it was soon no mystery how this five-foot-two ball of energy had twice been elected as her town's top administrative officer—not actually a mayor, given her town's form of governance, but fulfilling the same func- tions. The mystery, of course, was how she could possibly be failing to *effectively* cherish every molecule, every smile, of her adorable son.

Given my earlier meeting with Billy's father, Dianne Denver knew exactly why I had invited her to come to my office. In fact, her first words to me were something like, "So, you're the attorney for The Home for Little Wanderers. We send them a check for the children every Christmas. William told me that Billy had spoken with one of your social workers, and that you were following up with each of us. Obviously, we appreciate the opportunity to speak with you *directly*." Her emphasis on the word "directly" made it clear why she had agreed to come into my office: the last thing anybody wanted—especially a politician—was to deal with the Social Service authorities about how well they were parenting their child.

Since the odds of reforming Billy's father's emotive capacity seemed well south of minimal, I clearly had to make an all-out effort with the mayor—whatever it took. Our initial conversation, however, didn't go *quite* as well as I had hoped.

"Should I sugarcoat this or just tell you straight up?" I began.

"I can handle it," Denver replied with all the confidence you would expect of someone holding her office.

"Okay, then. Billy is trying to understand why he doesn't *feel* more loved by you and Mr. Denver."

The mayor was clearly taken aback but responded quickly. "You met his father; my guess is you already know the answer to that question."

"I think I do know half the answer, yes. But where do you figure in all this?"

"I love my son."

"Are you sure?"

"Of course I'm sure!"

"Then why isn't *he* sure?"

The mayor froze when I said this and sat perfectly still, speechless. I immediately realized that I needed to back down my assertion to something more palatable—I meant to be helpful, after all . . . "Mrs. Denver, let me rephrase that; I didn't say what I meant. Billy said he *knows* you love him. That's not in question for him. But he also said he can't *feel* your love. Those were his exact words. Why would he say that?"

Denver remained motionless, looking drained and sallow. And then, in the softest voice you can imagine, five little words seemed to sneak out of her mouth all on their own: "That's because I can't either."

"I'm sorry," I jumped in. "Did I hear you right? Did you say, 'That's because I can't either'?"

Denver looked down, crossing her arms over her chest while reaching up and putting her right hand over her eyes. She began to slowly massage her temples, seeming to contemplate how she wanted to respond. Then she just stood up, turned around, and walked right out of my office.

"Mrs. Denver," I called after her, "either you have this conversation with me, or I'll think seriously about advising my client to . . ." But long before I could finish my toothless threat, she was out my door and gone. Dianne Denver had called my bluff, and now I had no idea whatsoever how to proceed.

Fortunately, it turned out I didn't need one. Two days later, Billy called, and in the deepest, most serious tone of voice the ten-year-old could muster, he asked me to confirm that I had met with each of his parents. When I replied that I had, he reported that neither of them had mentioned their meeting with me, but that each had tried to connect better with him. And this, he concluded, "was just what we were aiming for. We're making progress." Billy reported that his father had discussed weekend camping plans with Billy, saying that he was really looking forward to spending some time together when Billy finished up with his treatments. This, Billy remarked, "is something my father hasn't suggested since I was quite young." I laughed out loud at his phrasing, and once again, the little guy had no hesitation at all in joining right in.

*

There's much, much more to this story: the legal work I ended up performing for the mayor presented enigma after enigma as it evolved, and even contained an element of adventure—a rare thing indeed. The chapters that followed in the case opened like a set of Russian dolls as I worked to resolve the legal issue in the mayor's past that disabled her ability to connect. The rest of the case story is available elsewhere,[31] but for our purposes, this abbreviated synopsis of the case illustrates how even the easiest love on the planet—the simple and direct loving of a parent for their child—can vary enormously depending on the quality of the connection between them. The misconnection between Dianne Denver and her son was a textbook example of an obstructed connection: she "loved" her child, and some-how she even "loved" that husband of hers. But her ability to fully connect with them, to make them feel loved, was compro-mised: her emotional resources were almost entirely centered on her own fears and anxiety from events in her past, leaving her only a peripheral capacity to connect with others.

In my law practice, such obstructed connections between parents and their children were by far the most common cause of chronic childhood loneliness. Many of the circum-stances that got in the way of nurturing and mutually reward-ing parent-child relationships were, not surprisingly, products of the social and financial difficulties so many families find endemic in today's economy. But there are many other factors that weigh heavily on the family bonds that are needed to keep children safe, to make them *feel* safe, and to allow them to fully develop the neural pathways of connection that they will need later in life to be nurturing parents themselves. Just to pick one factor from the scores we could each name: we live in a time when there is often significant geographical distance between the homes—and hence the lives—of family members.[32] This

---

31. J. W. Freiberg, *Surrounded by Others and Yet So Alone* (Boston: Philia Books, 2020).

32. According to the 2005 to 2010 Current Population Survey Geograph-ical Mobility Tables of the United States Census, between 2005 and 2010, 15.4 million people moved out of principal cities, while 11.0 mil-lion people moved in; suburbs had 17.9 million move in and 9.2 million move out. The Census also provides statistics setting forth the most common state-to-state moves in 2011: New York to Florida: 59,288; California to Texas: 58,992; California to Arizona: 49,635; Florida

geographical watering down of family ties—of connection—is new in human history: until the industrial revolution generated the development of today's massive cities, the vast majority of siblings and cousins lived near each other and interacted with one another throughout their lives.

Recent research has documented that this ever-increasing geographical mobility of modern life has had a particularly intense impact on the children of nuclear families who move substantial distances from their extended families and childhood friends. These studies show that this fallout varies for different-age children: young and latency-age children tolerate such change with modest impact, while teenage children can be severely impacted, with significant behavior sequelae.[33]

Intergenerational and intragenerational social mobility, and parental change in occupation and marital status, can place other types of obstructions between children and their extended families, or between children and their divorced parent. Part of the American dream—and not an insignificant part of the American reality—involves either upward social mobility or lateral occupational shift. While in many ways this can

---

to Georgia: 42,666; New Jersey to New York: 41,450; California to Nevada: 40,815; Georgia to Florida: 38,658; California to Washington: 38,421; and Texas to California: 37,087.

I want to share a personal example, as well. Both my mother and my wife's mother grew up in families with five siblings. In each case, these two families had been many generations in their two respective cities. And in each case, the five siblings had been enormously close with each other, and with their respective cousins, nearly all of whom remained in and around their city of origin—as most people did before World War II. Now of course, geographic mobility is the norm, and my wife and I don't live anywhere near any of our many cousins, who themselves are spread far and wide from one another. Though we each have strong feelings for our respective distant and dispersed families, it is a rare and exceptional matter for either of us to see any of our cousins— something that would have been substantially unimaginable merely two generations ago.

33. Anne E. Green and Angela Canny, *Geographical Mobility: Family Impacts.* (Bristol: The Policy Press, 2003).

be a good thing, there can be a steep emotional cost to leaving behind the family and friends one knew and cared for.[34]

Each of us could name a host of other current social phenomena that present obstacles to successful family connections. Drug addiction and its equivalents isolate affected individuals from family members, as do prolonged and structurally generated unemployment, high divorce and loss-of-custody rates, high imprisonment rates—and on and on. Many of these societal pressures affect adults in their role as parents, while at the same time placing direct pressure on the children of our era, who in turn exhibit their own ever-increasing connective dysfunctionalities. We see this in the geometric rise in attention-deficit/hyperactivity disorders, autism, and Asperger's-related illnesses in children, as well as in the tendency of today's children to substitute screen time for playtime.

One-Way Connections: Zachery's Case

While obstructed connections were the most common mode of misconnection that afflicted children in the cases that I reviewed for this paper, there were numerous other patterns of dysfunctional connection that plummeted youngsters into chronic loneliness—often despite their being surrounded by family, playmates, and schoolmates. The better part of a score of children, for example, were victims of a painful form of disconnection that I call "one-way connection." Let's take a look at one such case.

*

34. J. W. Freiberg, "The Truck Driver's Library," *Four Seasons of Loneliness: A Lawyer's Case Stories* (Boston: Philia Books, 2016).

About twenty-five years ago, Sue Lyons, the head of one of the smaller adoption agencies I represented, called to ask me to handle the legal work to finalize an adoption. In Massachusetts, children are placed in pre-adoptive homes for a mandatory six-month period before their adoption can be legally finalized, and that period was soon to be up for a little fellow we'll call Zachery. During this half year, as you might expect, social workers specializing in adoption matters are required by regulations to visit the pre-adoptive home on a regular basis in order to make certain that all is going well, and then to write a final report that is filed with the Probate and Family Court as an element of the legal finalization process.

Normally, I declined to do finalizations for the adoption agencies I represented because in acting as counsel to both the agency and its client, a conflict of interest would occur if ever a dispute were to arise. But in Zachery's case, I allowed myself to be talked into representing the adoptive couple, who we'll call Jane and Charles Sarnoff, principally because they were just weeks shy of their finalization proceeding when their attorney had been taken seriously ill. Lyons assured me that she couldn't imagine any conflict arising in the case, and practically begged me to help the couple avoid a delay of the adoption finalization hearing they were so looking forward to. So I relented.

It was immediately clear from the file Lyons sent along to my office that the Sarnoffs were an ideal adoptive couple. Charles Sarnoff owned a small but successful company that sourced "fasteners"—all those thousands of small parts that manufacturers need for their production lines. Jane, in turn, was a successful certified public accountant. They had tried every trick in the book to conceive a child—all to no avail. Subsequently, they had then turned to adoption to assure themselves of raising at least one child—and also in the hope that an adoption would serve as a magic fertilization charm, which, they told me, they had heard that it sometimes does.

The Sarnoffs owned a substantial home in one of Boston's suburbs, and they clearly possessed both the financial and the emotional resources to successfully raise a child. The home-study record couldn't have been more positive: there wasn't anything negative identified in their personal backgrounds, and their file was replete with rave reviews of their occupational success, their standing in the community, their close ties with their own families, and their many connections with a large circle of friends. They were a secular Jewish family, and they intended to raise the child in that tradition.

The entire finalization process could not possibly have gone more smoothly. Not surprisingly, Probate and Family Court judges relish the task of approving an adoption, which they typically do first thing in the morning before turning to a stress-laden day full of divorce cases, contempt proceedings, domestic restraining order issuances, and intra-family inheritance disputes. The Sarnoffs had requested that I ask the judge at the end of the proceedings if she would mind having a photograph taken with her holding the little baby boy, with me standing alongside her, posed with my briefcase. She was delighted to comply, and thirty minutes later, the three Sarnoffs and I walked out of the court building under a bright winter sky, shook hands, and went our own way.

Or so I thought. Just shy of a year later, Charles Sarnoff called and asked if I could come to dinner at their house the following week to celebrate the anniversary of the adoption. I was delighted to do so, and truly pleased to see how well Zachery the toddler was doing. Even better, Mr. Sarnoff told me that he had had a falling-out with his corporate counsel and asked if I would have any interest in serving as general counsel to his company. This ended up working out extremely well for all involved, and for about the next fifteen years, until the company was sold to a large competitor, it was my pleasure to provide the company's legal services, as well as serving as personal counsel to the Sarnoffs.

Zachery's childhood was just as Sue Lyons and her adoption social workers had predicted in their home study: he was a beloved only child who flourished in his supportive and attentive home. He excelled at school, and he grew into a handsome teenager with a magnetic smile. I was even invited to his Bar Mitzvah, where Zachery showed off his mastery of the Hebrew language as he read a passage from the Torah. Zachery was warm and friendly with me during the yearly celebrations of his adoption—as he reportedly was with everyone else he encountered. He seemed to be on a clear trajectory to college and a professional life, given his academic prowess and the consistent parental encouragement he received.

Then, quite suddenly, everything changed. In the last two years of high school, Zachery began drinking and using drugs to the point where it became increasingly problematic. While I saw his father less after the sale of the family company, as personal counsel to the family, I still had occasion to hear how poorly things were going. I learned that Zachery argued vehemently with his parents about anything and everything, renounced Judaism, and eventually dropped out of high school and moved in with a girlfriend.

Notwithstanding these developments, the Sarnoffs tenaciously and lovingly stuck by their adopted son throughout a veritable cascade of unpleasant chapters. Occasionally, there were brief but hopeful moments of recovery and abstinence; invariably, however, these were followed by relapse and ever-worsening decisions on Zachery's part. Progressively, Zachery made it clear that he would not be applying to college, and the Sarnoffs, although profoundly disappointed, accepted his decision. By this point, all they hoped for was sobriety and health. A year or two later, I learned that the skies looked somewhat brighter for Zachery: he had become an apprentice to a master plumber. Alas, this occupational opportunity was squandered within a year. Soon after that, Zachery informed his family that he had impregnated and married a woman who already had a child by an unidentified father. At the time of the marriage, Zachery's parents had never met his uneducated, non-working wife, let alone been invited to the wedding. Ouch.

*

When I was first asked to serve as counsel to several adoption agencies, it never occurred to me that this representation would be the source of some of the hottest and most virulent litigation experiences that would come my way. I distinctly remember thinking at the time that legal work involving adoption would involve nothing but sunny skies; after all, adoption is all about happy times for everyone involved, right?

On the contrary, I was to learn that adoption is an enormously complex psychological trek up a Mount Everest of emotion. This wasn't hard to understand when the adoption in question involved older children from abusive homes whose families lost or surrendered legal custody,[35] but it was also relatively often the case even for healthy newborn babies. There were several newborn adoption cases, for example, where underlying marital strife in the adoptive couple's relationship had been purposefully concealed from the social workers responsible for undertaking the statutorily required home studies. In all three such cases, the prospective parents had assumed that the arrival of a child would provide a common project and bring their fading love for each other back into full bloom. Ah, but that's what puppies are for, not children.

---

35. J. W. Freiberg, "The Loneliest Boy," *Four Seasons of Loneliness: A Lawyer's Case Stories* (Boston: Philia Books, 2016). Please see my discussion of the adoption of the "Doe" children in my story "The Loneliest Boy," which is discussed later in this paper as an example of a "dangerous connection."

Even in successful adoption cases—and I came to know quite a few—connection issues were not rare to find. One sees this, arguably, in the search for birth parents that so many adopted children undertake these days once they've begun their own adult lives outside the home of their adoptive parents. The jurisprudence controlling the availability of identifying information on birth parents was explosively volatile during the years of my law practice. When I first began my representation of adoption agencies, the statutory scheme in Massachusetts was straightforward and universally enforced by the courts: identifying information on birth parents could only be revealed to an adopted child (or in the other direction, to a birth parent) if the record contained two written, notarized letters permitting such disclosure—one from each party. Moreover, no person—not even a licensed adoption agency—was permitted to contact either party about their willingness to produce the second such letter: the controlling statutes and case law required a totally independent production of the written consent letters from both sides.

Then, bit by bit, judges began to substitute their personal views into the matter, presumably in response to changing societal norms about the wisdom and positive mental health benefits of "open adoption." Chaos followed, as you might imagine, with judges in adjacent counties—and sometimes even within a single court—ruling differently on identical disclosure petitions.

While the motivation to undertake such a search by an adopted child is easy to understand, take a moment to think about how the adoptive parents might feel when they learn that the grown child they adopted and raised is out searching for their birth parent. In recent years, more and more adoptive parents have had to learn to live with and, in some senses, "share" their adopted child with the child's birth parents. What impact might open adoptions have on the quality of the connection between adoptive parents and adopted children? Is the involvement of the birth parent by definition threatening to the adoptive parent? Should it be? The answers to these questions aren't really known yet: all this is so new. While recent published research has shed some light on these questions,[36] it will be years before the long-term effects of generalized open adoption will be fully understood.

But let's return for a moment to the Sarnoffs' experience, for it offers a window into the agony that can arise from a one-way misconnection between adoptive parents and the child they have raised and loved. What's interesting about the case, from our point of view, has nothing to do with Zachery's substance abuse. That sad phenomenon, as we all know, is in no way linked to the fact that Zachery was an adopted child: it is a national public health crisis of the first order that can emerge in a birth family as easily as in an adoptive family. Accordingly, let's assume, for purposes of this analysis, that Zachery's progressive involvement in addiction was in no way intended by him to be a rejection of his adoptive parents or their values.

What fascinates me about Zachery's case is something altogether different. There is, it seems to me, clear and convincing evidence that Zachery exhibited a pervasive and inexplicable rejection of the parental connections the Sarnoffs had worked so hard to build over the boy's entire childhood. The more the Sarnoffs adjusted their expectations and forgave Zachery for his failures, and the more they sacrificed financially and emotionally to help him climb out of his downward

---

36. Deborah H. Siegel, "Open Adoption: Adoptive Parents' Reaction Two Decades Later," *Social Work* 58, no. 1 (January 2013): 43–52. This sizable, long-term longitudinal study ended up showing no particular patterns of regularity among the adoptive parents. Most of the birth parent-birth child "reunions" were so temporary and emotionally minimal that they ended up being insignificant as stressors in the adoptive parents' lives. But the study is a good piece of work, even if what it ends up showing is what one would expect: the parent-child relationship is far more a matter of nurture than one of nature.

spiral, the more virulent became Zachery's rejection of all their efforts.

So, what evidence am I referring to? While there are other facts I could mention, the single most powerful piece of evidence, in my opinion, is Zachery's gratuitous announcement to his parents that he was "no longer Jewish." While most of us probably support the right of anyone to determine their own religious beliefs, affiliation, and practices, my assumption would be that most individuals who cease practicing the religion in which they were raised don't aggress their parents on the issue. I've known many lapsed Catholics, for example, but not one of them has ever thrown that in the face of their practicing parents. On the contrary, they report actively avoiding conversations about their beliefs and practice preferences.

To me, Zachery's apostasy is even harder to understand given that he is an adopted child whose only potential connections to *any* past lineage came through his adoptive parents. Family traditions and "roots" are psychologically important to each of us, so why had the Sarnoff family roots not become Zach's roots, especially given that he was brought up inside these traditions, given his religious training, his Bar Mitzvah, and the pride exhibited by his adoptive family at his accomplishments? What happened to all that parental love the Sarnoffs poured into this child?

I wish I had answers to these questions, but I don't. I remain completely flummoxed by Zachery Sarnoff, who, at least up to this point in his life, remains one of the bleakest examples that I have encountered of a one-way misconnection. That being said, Zachery's case raises one obvious question: Do adopted children have a higher instance of attachment disorders, or other psychological abnormalities? The answer is yes: empirical studies have documented some, if far from conclusive, evidence that an adopted person has an increased risk of certain mental health disorders including oppositional defiant disorder, attention-deficit/hyperactivity disorder, conduct disorder, major depressive disorder, and separation anxiety disorder.[37] Not surprisingly, therefore, adoptees are more likely than non-adoptees to have contact with mental health professionals.[38]

I do want to say, however, that I have known, both as counsel to numerous adoption agencies and in my personal life, beautifully adjusted, soundly connected, psychologically stable individuals who were adopted, or who were adoptive parents. The above discussion is only intended to state that there does exist evidence that there is some increase in the likelihood of untoward psychological ramifications coming from the break in biological family lineage that is by definition a part of adoption. Adoption involves disconnection, so it is hardly surprising that when the new family connections are grafted, sometimes they metamorphose into misconnections—even when everyone is operating in good faith.

*

In contrast to Zachery's case of one-way connection, I often worked on cases that involved the opposite dissymmetry: a child who sought a full-fledged connection with birth parents who, in return, exhibited only disinterest and disengagement. The parental detachment cases that I saw took many forms, and varied greatly in the degree to which the parents were emotionally uninvolved with their children and in the constancy of their disconnection. In some cases, the parental disinterest in

---

37. National Council for Adoption, *Adoption Factbook IV* (Sterling, VA: National Council for Adoption, 2007). "Adopted child syndrome" is a proposed but controversial term that has been applied to a host of behaviors in adopted children, including their elevated level of failure in bonding and attaching with others, not to mention statistics indicating the increased likelihood of their being defiant of authority figures and being arrested for teenage delinquency and truancy.

38. Ibid.

their children was inadvertent—a function of mental health limitations, drug and alcohol abuse, and the like ("obstructions," in my terminology). But in other cases, the rejection of the children was active and purposive.

Teen pregnancies were a prime source of such active rejection, as I came to know through serving as backup counsel for one of my law partners who was general counsel to one of Boston's major hospitals. This hospital, as is general protocol in all Boston hospitals, employed on-staff social workers who, among their many other duties, checked in with new mothers to ascertain that normal attachment was developing between a mother and her newborn. For obvious reasons, they kept an especially close eye on unmarried teens whose pregnancies were unplanned, or who identified no father, or whose life circumstances seemed unlikely to provide a sound basis for the many stresses of parenting.

I remember one of these cases with blinding clarity because when I was summoned to appear at the hospital in my law partner's absence, I had had no personal experience whatsoever with parental rejection of a newborn child. On the contrary, I was accustomed to the planned pregnancies of married adults who excitedly awaited the birth of their child. But my personal experiences proved to be entirely unlike their polar opposite: a depressed, unmarried teenager who had no relationship whatsoever with the man who had impregnated her, and no interest whatsoever in parenting a child. The social worker who had summoned me had determined that the new mother in question exhibited irreversible affective neutrality and a determined refusal to connect with her child. When the social worker asked the mother if she wished to keep the child or preferred to place the child for adoption, the young mother *immediately* agreed to put the child up for adoption— apparently, the idea had not previously occurred to her. It was clear that this teenage girl had no more affection for her child than any of us have for an item of trash we are about to discard.

When I left the room, I was so shaken by this experience that my ears were ringing. At the time, I was the father of an infant son who meant more to me than I could put into words—as he still does today, almost four decades later. While my mind didn't disagree that the young woman's circumstances made her decision a rational choice, my heart could in no way comprehend what she felt—or, more precisely, didn't feel. When I returned the following day with the documents of unconditional surrender for the young mother to sign, I warned her of the irreversibility of her decision—as the law required me to do. Ignoring what I had to say, she signed with no hesitation whatsoever. My hands were shaking so badly I had trouble affixing my notary stamp.

Before we pass on to the next category of misconnections—fraudulent connections—I want to just briefly mention unrequited love—a garden-variety one-way connection if ever there was one. It plays a major role in the lives of children—to the degree that it is hard to imagine that anyone reading these words passed through their teenage years without having fallen head over heels in love with a classmate who felt no mutual attraction whatsoever. And, of course, attorneys see the adult version of this in a goodly proportion of divorce cases: while one mate has completely disconnected from the marriage and is preparing for divorce, the other remains blissfully involved and is bowled over when the sad news of separation comes knocking at the door. One divorce plaintiff went so far as to ask me how he should go about breaking the news to his wife, who, he assured me, had no inkling whatsoever that he was already absent from the relationship—and had been for a number of years. As if I knew.

Fraudulent Connections: Anita's Baby

In the 1980s, Anita Adams was a doctoral student in art history at Boston College. She was "ABD"—a term that refers to a graduate student who has completed "all but [their] dissertation." Better still, her research project—which concerned Ancient Greek and Roman marble carving techniques—was well underway, and the outline for her book-length dissertation on the topic had been enthusiastically approved by her doctoral committee. In other words, everything was going swimmingly for Adams—until a two-foot snowstorm, an enticing invitation, and a fraudulent misconnection combined to change her life forever.

The morning after the storm abated, Adams found herself essentially trapped inside her tiny studio apartment by the massive snowdrifts the howling winds had left behind. Not a problem: it was perfect weather to plop down at her desk with a big mug of coffee and carry on with her work. No sooner had she begun, however, than the phone rang with what must have seemed like great news: it was her college roommate, who had read about the Boston storm and had called to rescue her. Anita found her friend's invitation to use the second bed in a Miami Beach hotel room absolutely irresistible, and twenty minutes later she was on the phone to see when she could book a flight from Logan Airport. Just three days later, Adams was sunning herself on a white-sand beach across the road from one of Miami Beach's picturesque, pastel-colored, art deco boutique hotels.

Two days into her trip, just shy of sunset on the beach, Anita crossed paths with an Englishman named Cedric Coulter. Ten years Adams's senior, Coulter was good looking in a sort-of-formal British manner. He was an impeccably well dressed, gentlemanly sort of fellow, and quite charming—warm, even—and extremely well spoken. On top of all this, Coulter owned a positively charming "Old Florida" wooden beachfront home a mile down the shore from Adams's hotel, and as if that weren't enough, he toured Adams around Miami Beach in his venerable, forest-green Morgan convertible. The one with the leather strap over its bonnet.

Coulter fascinated Adams with descriptions of his elite public school and Cambridge education in England, and his adventurous life of international trade, travel, and leisure. Best of all, Coulter seemed smitten with Adams, as unconcerned with her plain Midwestern looks as he was impressed by her prodigious knowledge of Ancient Greek and Roman marble statuary. Adams had dated before, but she had never, ever met an American boy who would listen to, let alone be open to sharing, her absolute fascination with art history. How in the world, she had asked Coulter, "could a sculptor possibly become skilled to the point where they could make hard, cold marble look as warm as flesh and as soft as cloth?" The vacation flashed by in a heartbeat, and Adams was crestfallen at having to return to snowy Boston.

Coulter, however, was not about to let a three-hour flight spoil their love affair: he flew up to Boston on alternate weekends, always taking the same luxurious suite in the Ritz-Carlton Hotel. A breakfast fit for royalty was brought to the room each morning on a rolling cart and served to the couple at an antique table that stood in front of a massive bay window that overlooked the Boston Public Garden. Newbury Street—Boston's premier shopping venue—was just a block away, and Coulter's delight in buying luxurious gifts for Adams knew no bounds.

By the end of the spring term, Adams's heart was won. In early summer, the two were married in an opulent wedding on the massive, sloping front lawn of a waterfront house Coulter had rented on Nantucket Island. Forsaking her graduate school career, Adams moved from her student life in Massachusetts to Coulter's lavish lifestyle in Miami Beach. For reasons that never became known to me, Adams simultaneously experienced a definitive break with her parents. Perhaps it was the age difference between the two lovers, or perhaps it was Adams's sudden cessation of her PhD studies, or perhaps it was the rush to marry—or some combination thereof. I never learned. But I do know that she was willing to pay that steep a price to join her life to that of this fascinating Englishman. Adams's lifestyle in Miami was, to quote her, "like in a movie." There were international guests, mostly from Latin America, and a constant stream of late-night parties fueled by fine French wines, catered gourmet meals, and abundant cocaine. Her new home came with a smoothly functioning staff: each and every mundane task of everyday life "just happened." Who could ask for anything more?

*

Roughly eighteen months after they moved to Miami, Coulter precipitously announced that his work—international business dealings that he had never fully described—called for a temporary move to Montreal. Adams was thrilled to leave the sweltering heat of a Florida summer, especially as she was now pregnant. And life for the couple in Montreal proved to be far more vibrant than it had been in Miami Beach: Coulter had rented a large flat in a sophisticated, artsy area of Montreal known as "Mile End." While Coulter dealt with his business matters, Adams—now, of course, "Mrs. Coulter"—spent her days practicing her college French in and around the art galleries, bookstores, and cafés that abounded in the lively neighborhood. The final two weeks of her time in Montreal were even more delightful: Adams had invited her cousin, Rita Carnes, to come up from Boston for a visit. Carnes had been a law client of mine for years, and it was through her that I was soon to meet Mr. and Mrs. Coulter.

The Montreal residency period ended when Mr. Coulter's business dealings once again required a precipitous move—this time to London. Adams was positively *ecstatic* at hearing this news. London was the home of the Elgin Marbles, and the British Museum housed a veritable treasure trove of ancient sculptural artifacts that were at the very heart of Adams's art history interests. Personal belongings were sent ahead from Montreal, as were other items from the now-empty Miami Beach residence which had been put up for sale. Travel plans for the couple were coordinated with Mrs. Carnes's return flight to Boston, with the Coulters to say goodbye at Logan Airport upon deplaning, and then to continue on with a British Airways flight to London. On the flight to Boston, the two cousins huddled together and made plans for Carnes and her husband to travel to London at Christmastime—by when there would be a baby to visit as well.

*

My introduction to the case began at about two a.m. on the night of the flight to Boston. Initially, it was my past client Rita Carnes on the line. That much I deciphered. Looking back, I've never been sure if it was my grogginess at the late hour, or Mrs. Carnes's inability to grasp and explain what the three travelers were experiencing at Logan Airport, but at the point when she handed the phone to Adams, I still had no understanding whatsoever of what the crisis was all about. At least I was fully awake, but even that didn't seem to help: Adams was so distraught and overwrought that the only thing I learned from her was that my legal services were being requested to deal with an emergency involving the police at Logan Airport. This was well before the advent of cell phones, and given what I could hear in the background, it was clear to me that I had been called on a phone line from police headquarters. I accepted the representation—still without any idea of what the circumstances were or what the case was all about—and did my best to calm Adams. In desperation, I asked her to pass the phone to one of the police officers, from whom I hoped to begin to gain some insight into what the hell was going on. The officer very nicely agreed to forward the call to his superior, who explained that while the Massachusetts State Police were holding Mr. Coulter, it was actually pursuant to federal and Florida state warrants. He knew nothing further but agreed to meet with me as soon as I arrived at Logan, and said that he would set out in the interim to learn as much as he could about what charges were involved.

About an hour later, after greeting Mrs. Carnes and meeting Mrs. Coulter, I met with a senior police official. The specific nature of the charges was still unknown to him, other than that there were multiple felonies involved in both the federal and Florida state warrants. In addition, while there were no warrants for the two women who had been traveling with Mr. Coulter, he asked that I volunteer to keep them at the airport until I was able to meet with the federal authorities in the morning.

As you might imagine, the five-hour interval between this meeting and the arrival of an assistant United States attorney felt like it took a month. The two cousins sat huddled up, reassuring themselves that whatever the error was that had been made, it would be readily resolved in the morning. I, on the other hand, passed the night studying half a dozen grant proposals that I needed to read through as a trustee of a charitable trust that funded graduate student research on the history of love. Yes, you read that correctly, on the history of love.[39]

---

39. J. W. Freiberg, "Professor Henry Huddleston and The History of Love," *Four Seasons of Loneliness: A Lawyer's Case Stories* (Boston: Philia Books, 2016).

But there was no error. And, as it turned out, matters were even worse than I feared. Way worse. In fact, after I met alone with the assistant United States attorney, I had the entirely unenviable task of reporting to Mrs. Coulter that there actually was no "Mr. Coulter." *He literally did not exist.* Her husband was, according to a number of entirely convincing documents that I had been shown, a completely different person from whom she had been misled to understand. He was an American named Michael Silber, so even his English accent was fake. The wealth Adams had experienced was neither inherited nor earned in complex international business transactions, as "Coulter" had represented. It was produced by his actual profession: he was a major drug dealer, involved in the importation of cocaine. This undoubtedly explained the many Latin American guests the "Coulters" had entertained in such grand style at the Miami Beach home. But drug dealing was just the beginning of Mr. Silber's legal problems: he had also been indicted in both jurisdictions as a coconspirator and accessory-before-the-fact in two drug-related, first degree murders. The only good news of any kind to report to Adams was that she was free to leave the airport: in no way did the authorities consider her to be involved as an accessory, including after-the-fact.

But all of this was only the beginning. A week later, I received a call from the criminal defense attorney to whom I had referred the case. He reported that he had come upon evidence that Coulter's marriage to Adams had been undertaken in bad faith—it was part of a failed scheme to avoid detection. And, given the content of one of the taped conversations to which this attorney had been privy, it was perfectly clear that his "love affair" with Adams, his proposal of marriage, and even his encouragement for her to conceive a child, were *all* part of his scheme to enter into an innocuous everyday life.

Nothing about Coulter's involvement in the relationship was real: every single element was purely fraudulent.

I will never forget Adams's reaction to my news. She was frozen by my words. She remained completely and utterly silent as I relayed item after item of Silber's fraud, her eyes and mouth all stretched wide open at the litany of horrors with which she was being confronted. When I finished, she remained perfectly silent, utterly stunned into stillness and speechlessness. This went on for two, perhaps three minutes. Then she began to shiver—lightly at first, and then violently. I bolted from the room to find Mrs. Carnes, whom I all but physically dragged in front of Mrs. Coulter, urging an embrace. Coulter rose from her chair to accept her cousin's bear hug, with Carnes having to lean in over the very pregnant belly that held Silber's—not Coulter's—child. I took the opportunity to repeat for Carnes what I had been told, as it was impossible to know with what level of accuracy Adams was going to retain any of the many details I had relayed. Then I packed the two of them into a cab that took off for Carnes's home—with Adams having remained entirely mute throughout the entire process.

Think of the damage done. Not only had Adams lost her husband—whoever he was—but also her child's father, her child's name, and half (or perhaps both halves) of her child's family history. She also lost every financial asset in her life: all of "Coulter's" assets of every kind were immediately seized and later forfeited as proceeds of his criminal activities. All that remained for Adams was what she had brought into the marriage—and given that she had long since disposed of her student clothing and most of her books, she basically had a closet full of clothes appropriate for a life she would no longer lead, and a used Selectric typewriter.

*

I want to briefly mention another case of fraudulent connection that shattered the lives of half a dozen people. Many years ago, an adoption agency client of mine placed a newborn baby girl in a pre-adoptive placement that seemed ideal. I never knew anything about the birth mother or birth family, nor about why they had relinquished their healthy little girl for adoption, as the couple had its own attorney for their adoption finalization. In such a setting, there was no role for agency counsel, so the case only came up on my radar once the head of the agency called to tell me that there was a serious problem.

When the agency had done its home-study visits to the household, everything had seemed in perfect order. The college-educated, middle-class couple kept a spotless home, and each held well-paying, stable jobs. The pre-finalization home visit had confirmed that all was well, and the couple had appeared ready, willing, and entirely able to proceed with the legal finalization of the adoption. I learned that when the couple had had their last meeting with the adoption social worker, they had sat on their couch with their arms entwined around one another, and that when the mother had held the child, the love and connection between the two of them had been, to quote the adoption social worker's written record, "entirely evident." The final line that the social worker had written in her home study summed up everything she understood to be the case: "I have never had an easier time giving my approval to an adoption finalization."

The only problem was, it was all a fraud. An hour before the call to my office, the pre-adoptive father had stormed into the adoption agency office with three deep, bloody gouges down his left cheek. He burst in on a meeting my client was having with one of her two adoption social worker employees, screaming that this was the third "fucking physical assault by my fucking wife," and that he and his attorney were headed to court that very afternoon to file divorce proceedings and swear out a domestic restraining order. He described to a shocked office that the agency's home study had never come close to piercing the surface of what life was really like in his home. That morning, he explained, he had snuck out of the house and packed the trunk of his car with the clothing and toiletries he would need to begin a new life, and that he had already rented an apartment and would not be returning home. Ever. More importantly for the agency, he revealed that he had never bonded at all with the baby, and that he would absolutely *not* go through with the adoption finalization—that's what he had come to announce, and what his divorce attorney had written in a letter that was slammed down on my client's desk. And then—to add insult to injury—he closed with, "But thanks for your hard work."

The first question the head of the agency asked me was whether, so late in the process, she had the power to do whatever she thought was best. My reply was simple: the agency had complete and plenary legal authority—even a duty—to do whatever it thought was in the child's best interests.

The next several hours were spent in collective deliberation trying to figure out just what indeed *was* in the child's best interest. This included a consultation with Dr. Evan Newsom, the chief of pediatric medicine at Boston Children's Hospital whom you may recall from Billy's case. In the end, the decision of the agency—based in significant part on Dr. Newsom's analysis of the level of domestic abuse in the household—was to remove the child from the pre-adoptive home, forthwith. Later that afternoon, I accompanied the agency's staff—along with a town policeman—to the pre-adoptive home and watched as the shell-shocked pre-adoptive mother learned for the first time that her husband would not be coming home that evening, and that he had told the agency he was filing divorce papers. Additionally, my client announced to the shell-shocked woman that her child was being removed by the adoption agency and would not be returned. Partway through this process, two of the adoption social workers had whisked the child out the door and were gone. When this dawned on the pre-adoptive mother, she immediately telephoned her own mother: apparently, her parents had purchased a house just two doors down the street to be near their only child—and only grandchild. I saw the wife and her parents over and again in court during the unsuccessful lawsuit they brought against my client, and I can assure you, there was little left of them by the time the judge ruled against them. They seemed mere shadows of themselves.

The child was placed by the Department of Social Services in an emergency foster care home the evening of the removal, and then presumably into long-term foster care after that; my client was no longer involved in the process, so I don't really know. I've often thought about that little girl, orphaned once by birth parents and a second time by a fraudulent misconnection. Just two years ago, I had the opportunity to watch my son and daughter-in-law hold my then one-year-old grandson, and the connection between the three of them was as powerful in its own way as the one-meter-thick steel cables that swoop down to suspend the Golden Gate Bridge from its massive towers that rise up from the rocks beneath San Francisco Bay. When I ask myself what it would have done to my little fellow's psychological capacity to someday connect securely and confidently with others in his life were he to have been ripped away as a one-year-old from his parents and placed with a series of total strangers—I can only shake my head in bewilderment. Studies on the topic, not surprisingly, have shown that children removed at tender ages from their mothers exhibit despair, apathy, and significant deficits in social responsiveness.[40]

40. Kimberly Howard, Anne Martin, Lisa J. Berlin, and Jeanne Brooks-Gunn, "Early Mother-Child Separation, Parenting, and Child Well-Being in Early Head Start Families," *Attachment and Human Development* 13, no. 1 (January 2011): 5–26. Hiram E. Fitzgerald,

*

Fraudulent presentation of self in relationships, of course, is not limited to the relationships of couples. "Jeffrey was a very nice neighbor" is the famous quote of Pamela Bass, who lived next door to the infamous serial killer and cannibal Jeffrey Dahmer. Or take another remarkably inaccurate assessment of another infamous murderer: "He was always sharing things with others, and overall was very friendly." These are the words of Eric Paddock, the brother of Stephen Paddock, who shot fifty-seven people in Las Vegas in 2017. Eric Paddock, obviously, had no idea whatsoever who his brother really was: "There is no reason we can imagine why Stephen would do something like this," the brother told reporters shortly after the mass murder event.[41]

Like Anita "Coulter," Pamela Bass's lack of insight into her neighbor and Eric Paddock's complete misreading of his own brother highlight extreme cases of fraudulent connections. On a more mundane level, many of us, I should imagine, have been taken aback when hearing for the first time about a divorce involving a couple who we had understood to be enjoying a solid marriage. And think about the hidden secrets that have come to life in recent years about very public persons. None of us, for example, had any inkling thirty years ago that hundreds, perhaps thousands, of Catholic priests were pedophiles who preyed on the children of their flock, and that the hierarchy of their church consistently covered this up, and hence

---

Tammy Mann, Natasha Cabrera, and Maria M. Wong, "Diversity in Caregiving Contexts," *Handbook of Psychology*, vol. 6. (Mahwah, NJ: Lawrence Erlbaum, 2003): 135–167. Michael Rutler, "Maternal Deprivation, 1972–1978: New Findings, New Concepts, New Approaches," *Child Development* 50, no. 2 (1979): 283–305.

41. CBS Interview of Eric Paddock (October 23, 2017). Katherin S. Newman, *Rampage: The Social Roots of School Shootings* (New York: Basic Books, 2004). This book provides a well-done discussion of how mass killers present themselves in everyday life.

enabled the predation. And how about the secret gay sex lives of some of the most virulent Republican antigay politicians, including US Senator ("wide stance") Larry Craig; Virginia US Representative Ed Schrock; Arizona US Representative Jim Kolbe; Maryland US Representative Robert Bauman; Florida US Representative Mark Foley; and California US Representative David Dreier. And one would think that the South Carolina voters who repeatedly reelected openly racist Strom Thurmond to the United States Senate must have been a tad taken aback to learn that he had fathered a child named Essie Mae Washington-Williams with a fifteen-year-old African American girl. Let's face it, people keep secrets. We all keep secrets.

What I am concerned with here, however, is when the hidden secret lies at the very heart of an interpersonal relationship—when the basis of the connection between two people is destined to fail precisely because one person's "secret" amounts to an outright fraudulent misrepresentation of who they really are, or why they are entering into the relationship. I never heard from or about Anita Adams again, but with a modest degree of certainty, we can deduce some things about the likelihood that loneliness and disconnectedness would find their way to her nameless, fatherless child.

Assume, for illustrative purposes, that Ms. Adams was never able to repair the breach that had occurred with her parents. What would it mean to raise a child with no roots or traditions reaching back along either parental line? Allow me to answer with an observation from everyday life. Just a few years back I delighted in watching my son hold the hand of that toddler grandson I mentioned above, reminding me of when I held my son's hand as he learned to walk, just as my father had once held mine. These connective links—the one in my family and the one in yours—go back to the very beginnings of human history. Our awareness of these chains of parental nurturing are part and parcel of what makes us human, and our experience of these connections is part and parcel of the process that forms the neural pathways that will enable toddlers in later years to successfully manage their connections with others. This, of course, is precisely what Dr. Amy Banks's studies have demonstrated,[42] and what she writes about so insightfully in her paper earlier in this volume. So, when a parent holds their toddler's hand as the child stumbles along taking its first awkward steps, the parent is teaching the child how to walk, for sure, but also how to connect—and thereby how to love.

With this in mind, I've often asked myself: What would Adams have told her child, once he or she was old enough to want to know—*to need to know*—who his or her father was? I could never see any way for her to escape the appalling dilemma in which she must have found herself at some such point. She could either tell her child that their father was a fraud and that she had no idea whatsoever about who he really was, or she could conjure up a fiction. Hardly an enviable choice. But no matter what Adams determined to tell her child, there is one thing of considerable psychological importance we know she could not possibly have told that child: anything at all about their father or their father's family.

When my son was young, he pressed me for stories of our family's past, just as I had asked my own father. From what I described, my son knew that his great-great-grandfather had immigrated to the United States from Germany in the early nineteenth century and worked as a cooper—a barrel maker. When I took my boy at about age ten to visit the Colonial Williamsburg culture park in Virginia, lo and behold, we came upon a fully costumed, working exhibit of the trade of cooperage. Two skilled coopers were busy carving the doubly arched

---

42. Amy Banks and Leigh Ann Hirschman, *Wired to Connect: The Surprising Science Between Brain Science and Strong, Healthy Relationships* (New York: Tarcher/Penguin, 2016).

staves that fit together to create watertight barrels and buckets—no simple thing. What surprised me, however, was the level of interest my boy displayed: we stayed in front of that exhibit for fully an hour while he plied the tradesmen with an unending stream of detailed questions. His intense interest stood in stark contrast to the hundreds of other tourists who passed by the exhibit during all that time: understandably, not one of them cast more than a passing glance at the cooperage display. Why the difference? Because, I would propose, my son was not just looking *at* the display; he was looking *back* at his family history, at his roots. Michael Silber's fraudulent presentation of his identity and family story denied his child any such link to his family's past, and as the poet wrote, "There are only two lasting bequests we can hope to give our children. One of these is roots, the other, wings."

Tenuous Connections: Victoria's Case

I found myself walking briskly back from court, trying like crazy to get to my office on time for a meeting with a new client named Victoria Bergeron. I knew nothing about Ms. Bergeron's matter, save that the telephone pink slip informing me of the appointment had borne the word—in all capital letters—"URGENT." Alas, as I exited the elevator, I was immediately informed by my firm's drill-sergeant–serious receptionist that I was late: my client was waiting for me in my office, while the gentleman who had accompanied her was using the washroom. Thirty steps later, I knocked on my own slightly ajar office door and opened it to find—*no one*. Or so I thought at first. It was only after I had rounded the two client chairs and my desk that I first laid eyes on my new client—one of the cutest little six-year-old girls you can imagine. I don't know what she thought about my sudden pop-up appearance, but I was stunned into silence—I had had no idea that my client was a child. But just then Victoria beamed a smile at me—an unforgettable, no-upper-front-teeth six-year-old smile. Her face was framed by silky, soft-looking brunette hair made up of a dozen different shades—and her eyes were so startlingly green that they seemed to be made of imperial jade. They absolutely beamed in the brightness of the daylight streaming in through the plate glass, floor-to-ceiling office windows that looked out over Boston Harbor.

We had just greeted each other when Jonathan Freeman, MD, knocked and entered. I assumed he was Victoria's father—certainly they treated each other as father and child. But I was soon to learn that their relationship was far more complex than that, and that the legal challenge facing me was to take steps to preserve the parent-child connection between the two of them that Victoria had known all her life, but that had recently been rendered exceedingly problematic and greatly at risk.

*

Dr. Freeman explained that Victoria's mother, Sandrine Bergeron, had recently suffered a completely unexpected fatal stroke. She had worked as a surgical nurse practitioner at Beth Israel Deaconess Medical Center, and that was the source of the referral to me—I'd served on the hospital's board of overseers for almost twenty years. The hospital was also the source of Dr. Freeman's relationship with Bergeron: he had moved to Boston for his residency in orthopedic surgery after attending medical school and finishing his internship in San Francisco. Within six weeks of first spotting Bergeron's eyes peering above her surgical mask as she handed him a scalpel, the two were deeply in love.

Sandrine Bergeron, Dr. Freeman continued, had held dual United States and French citizenship, as she was the daughter of a now-deceased French father and an American mother. Bergeron's mother was very much still living and could potentially make a claim for the custody of the child. She was, to paraphrase Dr. Freeman, "remarried to a rural Texas preacher who repeatedly saved the evangelical souls of the same half-dozen zealots . . . every Sunday . . . in a tent . . . in some tiny town . . . outside of Fort Worth, Texas." Sandrine, he explained, had had nearly no relationship with her mother, in part because "Preacher Man"—as he came to be called throughout the litigation that was looming—considered her the "devil's agent" for having had Victoria out of wedlock. This breach between mother and daughter was so extreme, Dr. Freeman reported, that there had been only one brief visitation from the grandmother a few weeks after the child was born. Apart from that, their only contact had been an irregular exchange of Hallmark cards.

Victoria was beginning to squirm a bit in her chair, which was so massively too big for her that her legs just stuck straight out. Using this as an excuse, I wondered out loud if she might have any interest in a cup of hot chocolate, and a few minutes later, she was off to the coffee room, hand in hand with the office librarian. Her absence was a palpable relief to both of us, as the obvious next topic was a description of the details of Victoria's paternity. The story Dr. Freeman told me was as follows.

Just a few months shy of seven years before the day we were meeting, Sandrine Bergeron had attended a two-week-long training session at Beth Israel, which is a Harvard Medical School teaching facility. There she had met and had an affair with a young Parisian orthopedic surgeon who had come over from France to attend the same session. After the Frenchman returned home, Bergeron discovered that despite the couple having used precautions, her period was late. It was during these same anxious days that Bergeron and Dr. Freeman first spotted each other in that operating room.

Dr. Freeman—a tall, bespectacled blond, whose gentle nature was evident in every movement or gesture that he made—went on to describe how his and Bergeron's relationship became serious within about six weeks of meeting one another. Then one evening, given that the topic of marriage had begun to come up in their conversations, Bergeron had sat him down to announce that not only was she pregnant by someone else, but that she also had no intention of even thinking about having an abortion.

Dr. Freeman, who became ever-more animated as he told me this story, said that he hadn't hesitated a moment before grabbing both of Bergeron's hands and astonishing her with his response: "That's fabulous! I'm as infertile as a stone, and I've been trying to figure out how to tell you!" The medical details followed: Dr. Freeman explained that he was a victim of hypogonadotropic hypopituitarism, which causes low pituitary gland output and the loss of germ cells in the testes. Since he had neither known of nor treated his condition in a timely manner, his infertility was permanent. That part I understood.

So, as the doctor summarized, "We were in love, she was pregnant, and I was infertile—everything was perfect." They pooled their money and bought a house on "Pill Hill"—a popular neighborhood for doctors in walking distance of the hospital. Bergeron had hoped that her new life, and especially her settling down with Dr. Freeman, would help patch up matters with her mother, but that was not to be—not with Preacher Man in the picture. Partly because Bergeron held out a glimmer of hope that somehow time and a grandchild would help heal matters with her mother, but mostly because of the couple's ridiculously hectic work and child-care schedules, Bergeron and Freeman had never gotten around to actually marrying.

My heart sank when Dr. Freeman told me this, and even more so when I learned what I feared might be the case: they had never approached an attorney to investigate permanency planning for Victoria, and hence had never even heard of a "stepparent adoption." Dr. Freeman looked borderline depressed when I described the easy pathway to permanency that they had forsaken: all they would have had to do, given that Bergeron had had sole legal and physical custody of Victoria, was to marry, file a petition for a stepparent adoption, and place legal notice of their intention in an appropriate newspaper. With this simple procedure, the adoption by Dr. Freeman would have permanently terminated Victoria's legal relationship to her birth father, whose name would have been replaced by Dr. Freeman's on Victoria's birth certificate.

Now, I explained, the circumstances were radically changed with Bergeron's passing. Dr. Freeman had no legal relationship whatsoever with the child unless—and I remember crossing my fingers as I asked him this, and wincing as he answered—they had taken some liberties with the truth and put Dr. Freeman's name on the birth certificate as the child's father. They had not.

There was only one further hope: disinterest on the part of the grandmother. At least the answer to this possibility was not yet known by Dr. Freeman. Incredibly, to my mind, the grandmother had not come to Bergeron's services and had been openly cold, even rude, to Dr. Freeman when he had called to tell her of her daughter's sudden and unexpected death. Apparently, Preacher Man had called out something like "serves her right" in the background—loud enough to be heard.

Just at this point, there was a knock on the door, and Victoria came skipping back into the room, her lips bearing admissible evidence that she had indeed enjoyed a hot chocolate. Clearly, we were done for the day, so we arranged to meet soon for another appointment, *sans* Victoria. I asked Dr. Freeman to make a list of every doctor, every teacher, every friend—absolutely everyone he could think of who would talk to me about the role he had played in Victoria's life. I also asked him to think about what strategy might work best with respect to the "g-r-a-n-d m-o-t-h-e-r," spelling out the word.

As they prepared to leave, Ms. Victoria leapt up into Dr. Freeman's arms and almost immediately fell asleep in the crook of his neck. The bond between the two was perfectly obvious, and I couldn't imagine a more worthwhile legal task than doing everything I could to keep the two of them connected.

I soon learned that we could gather a truckload of witnesses who would attest to the constancy of Dr. Freeman's loving co-parenting, and I had an expert witness in mind whose Harvard Medical School credentials would back up his testimony about the psychological calamity that could befall Victoria if she were removed from Dr. Freeman's loving care and custody. But the law cut the other way if the grandmother asserted her rights: we would just have to wait and see what she intended to do. "One step at a time" were my last words as Dr. Freeman carried his little treasure out the office door.

*

I set to work immediately. The first step was legal research, which, in the days before computer-aided case law inquiry, meant rolling up your sleeves and spending most of the night in the law library. I recruited an associate to help me, and by two in the morning, when we each had one of those hot chocolates Victoria had so enjoyed, all we could do was shake our heads back and forth at one another. Every which way we looked, controlling legal precedent blocked us: there was no way we could overcome the grandmother if she petitioned for custody of the child. Moreover, even if we could gather admissible evidence that the grandmother was for some reason demonstrably unfit to raise the child, we learned that that wouldn't help our cause: all it would accomplish would be to cause the court to grant legal custody of the child to the Massachusetts Department of Social Services. This, in turn, would mean that Victoria would flow into the Massachusetts residential and foster care system where, on average, children her age spend about thirty months before an adoption can be arranged. In such a scenario, Dr. Freeman's only chance of re-obtaining custody would be to sign up at an adoption agency behind a line of pre-approved couples who had waited for years with the hope and dream of finding a child to adopt. So, however you looked at it, under controlling jurisprudence, Dr. Freeman's relationship with Victoria was greatly at risk.

Dr. Freeman was scheduled to call me at home the following evening, and he did—at midnight—explaining that he'd been trapped in emergency surgery. I proceeded to explain that our legal research had confirmed our worst fears: whether or not the grandmother was fit to raise Victoria, if she filed an appearance in a Probate and Family Court custody battle, we would lose. Dr. Freeman was silent for quite a while absorbing the bad news and then phrased his response succinctly: "So, is it checkmate?"

I thought for a good fifteen seconds, and finally replied that I could see only one logical possibility, slight though it might be. There was, after all, one player in the world who could trump the grandmother: Victoria's biological father. I asked Dr. Freeman if he had any idea who or where the father was, other than knowing his name from Victoria's birth certificate, but his answer was a tragically sad "no." I went silent for at least another twenty seconds and then came back with a question that puzzled him: Does Victoria by any chance speak French?

And for the first time in the case I got a helpful answer: "Yes, she does. Perfect French. Her mother consistently spoke to her in French when I wasn't involved in the conversation, and so far as I could tell, Victoria is entirely bilingual—for a six-year-old."

Next question: Was he willing and able to spend some serious money to put on a full-court press in France to locate the father and to try to convince him to come to our rescue? His response was immediate: "Anything—every penny I have." I warned my client that there was exposure in this approach: if we talked the father into filing an appearance, and if the court indeed granted him custody, he could very well decide to take the child back to France. The good doctor's response was unforgettable: "If I can't raise Victoria, I'd sure as hell rather see her raised in Paris, France, than in Paris, Texas."

*

And so I dove in. From Victoria's birth certificate, we knew that her biological father was Dr. Henri Dagnaud, and we quickly learned that he was an orthopedic surgeon who lived and practiced medicine in Paris. Convincing him to help us, though, was an altogether more complicated matter. I told Dr. Freeman that, in my experience, there was no way such a monumentally complex paternity and custody arrangement could be discussed via telephone. Moreover, I explained, the initial presentation of the concept that I had in mind would be an extremely brittle moment—a moment when a quick "thanks, but no thanks" response could prove difficult to ever unfreeze. After all, to the best of Dr. Freeman's knowledge, Dr. Dagnaud had never even been told that his two-week-long dalliance with Sandrine Bergeron had resulted in a pregnancy. Clearly, the odds were that he would be both taken aback and not particularly delighted at the news. The negotiating challenge in such a circumstance, I explained, is to construct a strategy of initial presentation that minimizes the chances that Dr. Dagnaud would take a firm negative position before fully hearing us out. In practical terms, this meant that the discussion should definitely *not* take place over the phone—it needed to be in person, complemented by a set of enticing photographs of the lovely child, and presented in light of the fact that Dr. Freeman was willing to do the actual raising of the child, including funding all of the expenses of Victoria's upbringing.

Dr. Freeman showed no hesitancy whatsoever. This was the one and only child he would ever have, and he adored her. If our only winning strategy was to involve Victoria's biological father in order to overcome the grandmother's claim, then, by all means, he was willing to do so. Whatever it took. And given that Dr. Freeman spoke no French, he was crystal clear that it would be yours truly who would make the initial contact with Dr. Dagnaud—by whatever plan I could concoct that would raise the odds of a successful outcome.

It was at this point in our conversation that I realized that Dr. Freeman also needed to be present in Paris. The problem was, as back-up counsel to a major Boston hospital, I knew a little bit about how rigid and far ahead surgical schedules are planned out, and what relatively minimal backup coverage was available for absentee days. But either Victoria came first to him or she didn't, and I was completely certain that he needed to be part of the process. It was one thing for me to serve as an initial intermediary—lawyers serve that function all the time. But this was a complex negotiation that had to be closed in a fraction of the time Dr. Dagnaud should have been afforded to think things through from an emotional point of view. The only hope, it seemed to me, was for Dr. Freeman to be met, spoken with, listened to, and sized up by Dr. Dagnaud. And in French culture, this meant they needed to eat a meal together if we were to get anywhere. As I phrased my sudden revelation: "I can sell the qualities of a six-year-old child by photograph; a darling little French-speaking child is a darling little

French-speaking child. But I can't sell *you* by description or photograph. Dr. Dagnaud would be undertaking to work with you on this project for years to come—for the rest of your lives, really. It matters whether he finds you an enticing partner or not. You're both orthopedic surgeons—that's got to be a helpful connection, I would think. My guess is, how he thinks he can relate to you is going to be a very important element in his decision."

Dr. Freeman remained silent, taking all this in. So I jumped right back in when another idea struck me. "Look, genetically, Sandrine was half French. But culturally, what percentage French would you say she was in how she cooked, how she decorated your home, how she dealt with Victoria?"

The doctor fell silent for a few moments, thinking this through, before responding. "She cared a lot about her French roots, no question about it. And she was a super good French cook: Julia Child and Jacques Pépin were her favorite chefs, and there must be a dozen cookbooks in the house—most of them in French. And there are colorful faïence plates and copper pots hanging on the dining room walls, if that's what you mean. And I learned from her to eat cheese after salad and before dessert."

"Okay, say no more. You've been converted. Who knows; this may just work."

"Yeah, but one problem: I can't break my surgical schedule with so little notice."

"Doctor, you told me your number-one priority is to preserve your connection to your daughter. If that's true, I would ask you to think very carefully about whether you really want to pay me my hourly rate to argue with you about why you have no options here?"

A pause. A chortle. "Okay. Okay. But it'll be a hassle."

"And are Victoria's hugs worth a hassle?" I asked, and then, without waiting for his response, I added: "I'll send you my flight and hotel details as soon as I lock them in. Make your reservation for forty-eight hours after mine."

*

In the days that followed, it was time to plot out a strategy to meet Dr. Henri Dagnaud at a time, in a place, and in a manner that enhanced the odds that he would at least listen to our proposal. As you might imagine, the beginning of formulating any such strategy is to research just who you are dealing with, and so I asked my office's private eye, Reginald Brooke—"Longfellow," as he was always called—to use his European contacts to come up with a Paris-based investigator who could learn as much as possible, as quickly as possible, about Dr. Dagnaud's personal and professional circumstances.

Within three days, Longfellow called back to say he had located the perfect spook—a Parisian private eye named Laurent Fauvet—fully licensed, and with appreciable experience. I spoke with this gentleman the following day, retained his services, and just a week after that, I received his initial feedback. Dr. Henri Dagnaud practiced orthopedic surgery at Hôpital Cochin near Boulevard du Montparnasse in central Paris. He was a respected professional who also taught classes in surgery at the University of Paris medical school, and he had recently published a book with two colleagues that introduced and refined new techniques in arthroscopic hip replacement. And—no surprise here—his résumé mentioned that he had once attended a two-week-long training at Beth Israel Deaconess Medical Center/Harvard Medical School. As far as Monsieur Fauvet could ascertain, that was the only time Dr. Dagnaud had ever traveled to the United States. He was married and the father of a young daughter. (I remember wincing at hearing this.) He and his wife, a journalist named Sophie Bernard, owned an apartment near Luxembourg Gardens, and also a small ski cabin in the Hautes-Alpes not far from Annecy. There was nothing whatsoever on the negative side of the ledger: no lawsuits, no criminal matters, no financial troubles.

In my experience, initial approaches to an unknown party like Dr. Dagnaud failed or succeeded on the quality of the approach strategy: I had seldom seen strong tactical maneuvers make up for an ill-conceived strategy. So finding just the right approach was critical, probably even pivotal. The one and only card I had up my sleeve that I could think of was my involvement with the board of overseers of Beth Israel Deaconess Medical Center—which, of course, is where Dr. Dagnaud had met Sandrine Bergeron. After a fruitless week spent trying to devise an approach that did *not* take advantage of this link, I gave in, called Dr. Freeman, and asked whether there was a lecture series or some equivalent forum to which Dr. Dagnaud could possibly be invited. Later that same day, Dr. Freeman returned my call, reporting that this was not a problem at all: it turned out that Dr. Dagnaud's recent book had generated a fair amount of acclaim, and he would be entirely welcome to give a talk in the Department of Orthopedics—if the hospital administration was in agreement, and if I would provide simultaneous translation. So, after all this was lined up, I called Dr. Dagnaud's administrative assistant in Paris to explain that I would be coming to Paris in order to extend a Harvard Medical School–linked invitation to him. Two days later, I learned by return call that he had accepted to meet with me. I asked if we could meet for lunch to discuss the lecture— and the assistant suggested a bistro down the street from the hospital. The scene was set.

*

And so it came to pass that just shy of two weeks later, I stepped off an Air France jet at Charles de Gaulle Airport and headed for a small boutique hotel near the Place de la Contrescarpe in the heart of the Latin Quarter—walking distance from the Hôpital Cochin. It was a typical Paris fall day: gray, with the cobblestones underfoot seeming as if they were permanently wet—recent rain or not. They gave off a chill and a stony odor that I have always associated with the city since first spending a year there as a graduate student in the 1960s.

The morning seemed endless the next day as I awaited the luncheon meeting. I had no way to predict Dr. Dagnaud's reaction, and I couldn't quiet my fears that he might just get up and leave the table. Denial, as we all know, is not the world's rarest reaction to the appearance on the horizon of troubling news. Finally, promising myself that I would walk slowly, it was late enough to leave for the restaurant—a simple but classic bistro on Boulevard du Montparnasse.

Fifteen minutes after my early arrival, the maître d' approached the table, announcing the appearance of my luncheon companion—obviously well known to him. At forty, Dr. Dagnaud was in the prime of life: he was what the French call *"un bel homme, bien dans sa peau"*—a man who is handsome, in part because he is at ease with himself. Like so many Frenchmen, he was still lithe, with the build of a downhill skier. He wore his salt-and-pepper black hair combed back and sported just the asset I had dreamed of finding: the same jade-green eyes that Victoria had amazed me with that first day in my office.

Having plotted out my strategy in detail with friends the evening before, I knew where I was heading. After a minimum of pleasantries, I began the process of admitting to Dr. Dagnaud that I had invited him to our meeting on somewhat false pretenses. As I spoke, I simultaneously opened a folder of photographs and slipped out a strikingly beautiful eight-by-eleven photograph of Sandrine Bergeron, his lover of some seven years in the past. It froze him. He just sat there with a softer-than-cotton smile, making quiet "umm" sounds deep down in his throat, lost for the moment in what must have been delicious memories. He never once looked up at me as I began to quietly narrate what had befallen Sandrine after their two weeks together in Boston: her discovery of her pregnancy, her decision to handle the matter on her own, and her extraordinary good luck at meeting another wonderful man who was perfect in every way for her—even for her circumstances. I explained how he would have never heard again about what followed in the wake of his visit to Boston, save for Sandrine's completely unexpected and sudden death, and Dr. Freeman's desperate need for his cooperation in order to maintain—or share—custody of the child. Then, after a pause so long that it amounted to an insistence that he look up at me, I began to slip him photographs of beautiful little Victoria—beginning, as you might well imagine, with the one that best displayed her set of their shared imperial-jade-green eyes.

Complete silence came over the table. I gave Dr. Dagnaud all the time he wanted to absorb how the child's looks reflected a mix of his and Sandrine's. Only after a goodly pause did I dare ask if he and Sandrine had stayed in touch after his return to France, and he answered that they had done so for several weeks, with a profusion of potential follow-up ideas. But then, he added, the correspondence had ended precipitously. "It probably was the pregnancy. God, I wish she'd told me. Who knows what we could have worked out." I allowed the silence that followed that remark to carry on just as long as he wanted.

Dr. Dagnaud finally broke away from his own reveries to ask about details of the legal status of Dr. Freeman's relationship to the child, which gave me the perfect opportunity to explain how we desperately needed him to support our efforts to keep the child with Dr. Freeman. "My idea is that the child would be raised in Boston while young, and later, as you and Dr. Freeman would work out between you—with perhaps a high school year spent here in Paris; who knows—whatever the two of you work out in the years to come. That way, she could benefit from both languages and both cultures. So, depending on what you thought best, if you agreed, we could all recommend to the court that in the early years, your involvement would be just an occasional visit. And, Doctor, please understand that Dr. Freeman is very clear on one point: he intends to pay one hundred percent of all the expenses of raising the child. He doesn't want this to be a financial burden on you or your family in any way, ever. He doesn't care about the money at all; all he cares about is being able to raise this child. He'll never have another one—he is completely infertile."

I was waiting for a response to some of the specifics I had laid out, but all Dr. Freeman said—in a dreamy, far-away tone of voice—was: "Her eyes!"

I jumped on this remark—far too indiscreetly. "Aren't they remarkable? It was the first thing I noticed about her . . . I can't tell you how lovely this child is. I spent half a day with her recently. We spoke about how I was going to go meet another daddy for her, and if everything worked out right, she'd have two daddies to keep her safe. She would be a jewel in your life, Doctor, a big sister to your other little girl."

Dr. Dagnaud furrowed his brow at my having carelessly divulged personal information that he knew he hadn't shared with me. While I couldn't tell how much he made of my slipup, he almost simultaneously made it clear that our meeting was over—without our even having ordered any lunch. "Counselor," he said in a sincere tone of voice, "it looks like this little girl is coming into my life whether I do it with grace and an open heart, or whether I struggle around trying to weasel out. Assuming a DNA test confirms what seems obvious to me from her eyes, I'm pretty much convinced this is the way to go. But let me be clear with you: the issue will be my wife. Give me a day to think through how we introduce all this to her; I assume I can take the photos, no?" I nodded yes, although I pointed to the one of Sandrine, adding, "You might want to think twice about taking this one."

"Good point," he replied, slipping it back across the table. "I'll need your help for sure in introducing this. And understand one thing: I have never talked Sophie into anything, ever. She has to get there on her own. Always. That's the difficult issue here. Call me at my office in the morning."

"I'll do just that," I answered, trying not to let my excitement show. "And by the way, Dr. Freeman arrives tomorrow morning. My dream is that we could all get together and have some preliminary discussions about where this could possibly head. You're a remarkable man, Doctor, for letting me present the situation with such . . . calm. Thank you."

Dr. Dagnaud's last words as he stood and pushed in his chair were sobering: "There are a number of gates here for us to ski through, Counselor; we'll see if we're still on the same *piste* in the coming day or two." And with that, he was gone.

*

Every single connection in Victoria's life was at risk: her ties to Dr. Freeman, her bonds to his family, her links to all of her school and neighborhood friends, and her involvement in the vibrant life she knew in Boston. While she was too young to appreciate the profundity of the many losses she potentially faced, we became increasingly convinced that she had a pretty good idea that life as she knew it hung in the balance. One thing we knew she understood all too well: what loss was all about. Her mother had just disappeared one day, never to return. The hard edge of reality that the custody trial would pose was whether the man she knew as her father would be lost to her as well.

*

Once again, the brief space available in this essay does not provide the space for a full description of how Dr. Freeman's deft
hand on the jazz piano turned the tide in our favor in Paris,
bringing Dr. Dagnaud's wife fully into the project. Nor is there
space here to allow for a description of the fascinating week-
long custody trial that ensued, with its equally convincing and
yet diametrically opposed expert witnesses, and its stream of
fact witnesses testifying to the ready, willing, and able parenting—or grandparenting—that could be supplied by either side
of the family. Those interested can find the full case study presented elsewhere,[43] but I can't resist sharing with you just one
astonishing moment in Victoria's case: how she unexpectedly
became the star witness at trial.

At the time I decided to put her on the stand, we were—it
seemed to me—losing the trial. Opposing counsel had done
a brilliant job of arguing that Dr. Dagnaud's involvement in
the trial was borderline fraudulent in that it had been arranged
by me to trump the grandmother's bloodline link to the child.
(Guilty as charged.) And, as you might imagine, he also made
note of the fact that Dr. Dagnaud had himself testified—via
translator—that his involvement would be modest during the
early years of the joint-custody arrangement. (Perfectly true.)
And then there was counsel's oft-repeated line to the judge:
"Obviously, Your Honor, the bulk of the raising of young
Victoria is going to be handled by Dr. Freeman—or, more
accurately, by some nanny he hires—not by Dr. Dagnaud. Dr.
Freeman is not a blood relative, Your Honor. This all makes no
sense."

My assessment going into the final day of trial testimony
was that we needed to get the judge's mind away from the

---

43. J. W. Freiberg, *Surrounded by Others and Yet So Alone* (Boston: Philia
Books, 2020).

unhelpful jurisprudence that complicated our efforts and to connect him with Victoria on an entirely more immediate level. The one and only idea I had for doing this was to put the little six-year-old on the stand—both to put in the record that she was bilingual, and to let the judge see this thriving child up close.

And so, I called Ms. Victoria as a witness. She proceeded to climb on the witness chair and *stand on it* in lieu of sitting—entirely her own idea. This was very clever, actually, as it put her little face on the same level with the judge's face. But this was just the beginning: to my complete and utter surprise, she had no sooner been sworn in when—completely on her own—Victoria asked the judge if her biological father, Dr. Dagnaud, could come over to the judge's bench, since she wanted to show the judge something. His Honor—whose hard surface gave its first hints of melting in the presence of this little Shirley Temple ball of energy—"suppose[d] so, unless Attorney Torpor has an objection." He didn't dare. Dr. Dagnaud walked up to the side of the bench next to the witness chair, and was instructed by Victoria in no uncertain terms—in French: "Lean close, Papa; put your face next to mine." He did just that, and then both leaned in over the end of the judge's bench toward the judge, their two cheeks almost touching, not more than four or five feet from His Honor. "What do you see?" asked Victoria.

"Um, two faces, two very nice faces," Judge O'Connor replied, sounding a bit stumped by the exercise.

"No, no," scolded Victoria. "Look at our eyes."

There followed ten seconds of stunned silence before the judge did just what Victoria had apparently plotted and planned: "Oh my goodness, they're identical! And so green—I've never seen such green eyes . . . Ahem . . . Um . . . Um . . . Thank you, young lady, a very good point you've made indeed. Now everyone back to their place."

It took a moment for the courtroom to settle, and for me to catch my breath. I couldn't believe what a hugely big move this tiny little girl had just engineered—without the first thought of mentioning it to me.

*

With your indulgence, my reader, I am going to refrain from including the outcome of the trial in this brief synopsis of the case—precisely because the resulting uncertainty you might feel underscores what this category of misconnection is all about. And I would ask you to go even further, if I might. Put yourself in Dr. Freeman's shoes for a moment: imagine learning that *you* might lose custody of the child or children in your life—or the company of somebody else you dearly love. Arguably the next worst thing to actually losing the company of someone beloved is living in constant fear that that might happen. It was not rare for me to work with clients who lived with such uncertainty about the permanency of their connection to those they most cherished, and several described in detail how this colored every second of their waking day and terrorized their dreams at night. Human consciousness is very much unlike that of other animals—they live only in the present, whereas we bring our expectations, hopes, and fears of the future into our present. This means that those clients of mine who experienced their principal connections as tentative or provisional or temporary or conditional or erratic—clients who could not trust the robustness and permanency of their interpersonal relations—often *already* experienced themselves as disconnected, even before there was actual rupture and detachment.

As you might expect, the interpersonal behavior patterns of these anticipatorily lonely clients often generated negative spirals, infecting and degrading what was left of the relationships they most cherished. One such case involved an architect who well understood that his hard-fought and well-deserved divorce from a hellion of a woman would lead her to lobby their grown children to stop seeing him. This gentle, good-natured man experienced such angst over this that it led him to seek a constant stream of verbal assurances from his children that they would hold firm against the expected onslaught. While the children spent the first few postdivorce years attempting to reassure him, there came a time when, one by one, they pulled back in reaction to his disquiet, leaving him feeling ever-more disconnected and emotionally adrift, and progressively more in need of the verbal assurances that his children were increasingly loath to give.

Another case in this category involved an African American woman who, despite her better instincts, had agreed to marry a Caucasian man whom she adored—but whose family was deeply uncomfortable about their union. Despite her in-laws' reportedly good faith efforts to learn and grow in this respect, when the couple had a relatively mild falling-out in the seventh year of their marriage, all the racial tension that had been kept below the surface spewed forth volcanically from the husband's parents. This rendered reconciliation all but impossible, and significantly compromised the relationship of the couple's two children with their paternal grandparents. My client reported that throughout her marriage—from day one— she had experienced a disquieting and ever-present anxiety about the durability of her marriage and that her angst played out in frightening nightmares.

Dangerous Connections: Seth's Case

While each of the modes of misconnection we have examined so far can cause both emotional distress and operate as a factor in generating or exasperating somatic disorders, there is a final category of misconnection that can be actively dangerous, even perilous. To discuss this type of defective connection, let's take a close look at the incest reported in the first story in this edited collection, "The Loneliest Boy." Incest, after all, is arguably the single most dangerous misconnection that there can be, or ever has been.

Dangerous misconnections are complex in nature because of the dynamic balance that exists between what is exquisite (the connection) and what is abhorrent (the danger). Dangerous connections, accordingly, are entirely distinct from situations where there is only danger—and no connection. In a hostage situation, for example, you have only danger: a collection of entrapped people in peril, who have no connection to their captor—nor to one another.[44] Contrast this with a clear example of a dangerous connection, such as domestic abuse. Social workers and clinicians have often reported the difficulty they experience in convincing battered wives to leave their abusive husbands.[45] While at times (or in part) this reluctance is simply a reflection of the successful colonialization of the mind of the battered spouse by their psychologically dominant mate, at other times the failure to escape can be (or be in part) a

---

44. Prolonged hostage situations have occasionally led to the "Helsinki syndrome" or alternately, "Stockholm syndrome," where a hostage begins to identify and make a connection with his or her captor, entering into something closer to a "dangerous connection," as I use the term. Perhaps the best-known American case of this was when the newspaper heiress Patty Hearst developed enough connection with her Symbionese Liberation Army captors that she agreed to join them in a subsequent bank robbery. One of the best studies of this phenomenon, however, is a fictional treatment: Ann Patchett's *Bel Canto* (Harper Perennial Modern Classics, 2005).

45. Ann Goetting, *Getting Out: Life Stories of Women Who Left Abusive Men* (New York: Columbia University Press, 1999); Albert R. Roberts, ed., *Helping Battered Women: New Perspectives and Remedies* (New York: Oxford University Press, 1996); Rachel Louise Snyder, *No Visible Bruises: What We Don't Know About Domestic Violence Can Kill Us* (New York: Bloomsbury Publishing, 2019).

function of the love and loyalty the battered spouse still feels for their battering mate. Love is a complicated thing: I have had clients who remained in love with child-abusing spouses, alcoholic spouses, drug-addicted spouses, gambling-addicted spouses—and even domestically abusive spouses.

Incest, in some ways, is the most extreme example of a dangerous connection because it involves the combination of maximal connection (family) with maximal danger (Class C felony and generalized social expulsion). While the definition of incest varies from state to state in the United States,[46] and even more so from country to country,[47] most states classify

---

46. Massachusetts, the state where the case profiled in "The Loneliest Boy" took place, defines Incestuous Marriage or Sexual Activities, Massachusetts General Laws Chapter 272, Section 17 (2013), as follows: "Persons within degrees of consanguinity within which marriages are prohibited or declared by law to be incestuous and void, who intermarry or have sexual intercourse with each other, or who engage in sexual activities with each other, including but not limited to, oral or anal intercourse, fellatio, cunnilingus, or other penetration of a part of a person's body, or insertion of an object into the genital or anal opening of another person's body, or the manual manipulation of the genitalia of another person's body, shall be punished by imprisonment in the state prison for not more than 20 years or in the house of correction for not less than 2½ years." Alabama's statute, in contrast, only disallows marriage or sexual intercourse, and the defendant must know of the familial relationship: Alabama Code Title 13A, Criminal Code 13A-13-3, reads: "(a) A person commits incest if he marries or engages in sexual intercourse with a person he knows to be, either legitimately or illegitimately (1) His ancestor or descendant by blood or adoption; or (2) His brother or sister of the whole or half-blood or adoption; or (3) His stepchild or stepparent, while the marriage creating the relationship exists; or (4) His aunt, uncle, nephew or niece of the whole or half-blood."

47. With reference to incestuous relations other than marriage, European countries vary widely: some allow incest between consenting adult siblings (Spain, the Benelux, and Portugal); France provides an interesting historical case: the 1810 penal code promulgated by Napoleon I and adopted throughout most of Europe abolished incest laws in France, Belgium, and Luxembourg. But in January 2010, France reinstated laws against incest. The new law, however, defines incest as rape or sexual abuse on a minor "by a relative or any other person having lawful or de

incest as a Class C felony. Other Class C felonies include kidnapping, arson, sexual assault, second-degree murder, and robbery—undeniably serious felonious crimes. But incest, of course, is more than a crime: it is also a moral transgression of the highest order—even if it is committed unwittingly, as in the foundational Greek myth *Oedipus Rex* where, unknowingly, Oedipus marries his mother, Jocasta, and has four children by her.[48]

*

In this general framework, let's take a look at the unique instance of dangerous connection found in the incest that lay at the heart of Seth and Ashley's case. As you may recall, the two siblings were raised in a biological home with "the most extensive child sexual abuse" known at that time to the Department of Social Services, to quote its then general counsel. The boundaryless and rampant sexuality in the family took place over three generations: the two children were sired by their

---

facto authority over the victim." In other words, incestuous relations between consenting adults is not prohibited). In other European countries, especially Scandinavian countries, incest is strictly illegal (Denmark, for example). Interestingly, in Germany, incest is currently illegal, but in September 2014, the German Ethics Council recommended that the government abolish laws criminalizing consensual incest between adult siblings, arguing that such bans impinge unnecessarily upon citizens. African countries vary as well: some allow consensual incest between adults (Ivory Coast), while others punish it by death (Zimbabwe). Latin America has significant variations from country to country (Argentina and Brazil have no criminal punishment if the involved are over the age of consent, whereas in Chile such activities are strictly illegal). Asia shows similar variations (China, Thailand, and Japan allow incestuous sexual activities between consenting adults, whereas in Vietnam such activities are illegal. The Indian Penal Code does not contain any specific provision against incest, but as in the substantial entirety of countries, there are protections against the sexual abuse of children.

48. Donald L. Wassen, "Oedipus the King," *Ancient History Encyclopedia* (January 2018).

step-grandfather, who had an active sex life not only with his wife (the children's biological grandmother) but also with all three of her children, one of whom became their mother. These two children were only toddlers when the step-grandfather began his sexual assaults on them, at times accompanied by their grandmother, aunt, and/or uncle. Basically, so far as we could discern, there were no sexual boundaries of any kind in the household.

There was, of course, very grave danger associated with this unbounded incest, and we know that the father/step-grandfather was acutely aware that any communication of the family's sexual activities to the outside world could lead to devastating results. Accordingly, he took steps to lessen the likelihood of a leak by the children about the sexuality in the household. For both the consulting psychiatrist on the case, Dr. Richard Putnam, and for me, one of the most fascinating challenges of the "Doe case" was our struggle to discern just how the father/step-grandfather was so successful in obtaining perfect compliance of the children with the family's code of secrecy.

After two solid years working together on the legal and forensic aspects of the case, including reading thousands of pages of documents and deposing scores of witnesses, including the children for three full days each—and after Dr. Putnam's three two-hour psychiatric examination sessions with each child, we concluded that there were two principal factors that allowed this secret society to operate so success-fully for so many years.

First, the secrecy campaign engineered by the father/step-grandfather *refrained from frightening* the children with warnings about how they would be removed from the house if they disclosed the sexuality. In contrast, the typical approach that sexually abusive parents use is to repetitively threaten their children that if they ever slip up, the police would come to arrest the parents and send the children off to reform schools. This threat, *in and of itself*, is an extremely powerful psychological stressor to a young child, because it amplifies a child's single biggest fear: loss of their parents' provision of shelter, sustenance, and nurturing. The very presence of the threat, in other words, means that such children are encouraged to conceptualize their worst fear: that their most critically important connections are tenuous and at risk. This, in turn, is likely to cause such a child to feel unsafe, and it is precisely when children feel unsafe at home that they tend to disclose (or confirm to questioning adults) their concerns and worries. So what was clear to us both was that we needed to learn how the father/ step-grandfather avoided this dilemma.

Second, apart from the boundaryless sexuality, we learned that the adults in the Doe family were nurturing and caring toward the children. It wasn't easy to admit this to ourselves, given what was going on sexually, but in the end, we had no choice: there was bountiful and uncontradicted evidence that the children were properly and lovingly fed, clothed, housed, helped with homework, taken regularly to doctors and dentists—everything the rest of us do for our children. It's also important to mention that, so far as we could learn, the incestuous sexuality in the parental home never involved physical pain to the children: most importantly, the sexuality never involved penetration or other sexual acts that necessarily would have involved pain and discomfort. In the civil lawsuit that followed the disclosure of the inter-sibling incest in the adoptive household, we deposed every single teacher, doctor, nurse, dentist, and social worker who had treated or worked with Seth and Ashley in their birth home, and *not one* of these professionals ever picked up on one single hint—*even looking back with twenty-twenty hindsight*—about the birth-home sexuality these children were experiencing and concealing.

One thing we learned for certain: the children felt motivated to protect their home life—in part because they reported that their home had been *fun* to be part of. When we deposed the two siblings—for three full days each—we had ample time to explore their take on the sexually infused, cultlike connection between them and their family members, and there was no doubt that they found their home life a good deal more satisfying than was comfortable for us to hear, conceive of, or acknowledge. Below, from a deposition transcript, is Seth's description of what general family life was like for the children. What is relevant for us in this selection is the picture the boy painted about the *tone and tenor* of what life was like in the birth home:

> When I was holding Ashley, it was . . . how I got back to my family. It was as if I could actually feel and hear and smell the family all around me again, like when we had dinner with everyone sitting around the table eating and laughing . . . It was loud, it was crazy, it was funny—and it smelled good. Once my dad spilled spaghetti sauce on this clean shirt, and after he looked down at the mess, he looked up and said how stupid he felt. We always put on clean shirts for dinner, but you know what we all did? Every one of us started smearing spaghetti sauce on our shirts too, and then all over our cheeks, and we all laughed so hard and so long that we all had tears running down our cheeks making tracks in the spaghetti sauce.

After two years and countless hours of conferencing between us, Dr. Putnam and I felt that we had finally arrived at an understanding of how the absence of fear and the presence of connection probably explained both the lack of disclosure by the children, and the failure of insight by any outside professional. But this still left us with an unanswered question: Why didn't the incestuous and age-inappropriate sexuality denigrate or detract from the character development of the children? Remember, as I emphasized in "The Loneliest Boy," all twelve attorneys on the case and Dr. Putnam—all thirteen of us, *without exception*—found the children to be not only psychologically intact but also warm, open, and engaging youngsters. How was this possible? What protective mechanisms had been at work? What had sheltered these two children from being psychologically diminished or frightened—either by the sexuality itself or by its potential real-world consequences if ever the outside world were to learn of it?

We concluded that the operative variable was the depth and sincerity of the *connection* the children felt to their wild, crazy, loving, sexually boundaryless family. Remember, dangerous connections are not only about danger; *they are also about connection.* We came to learn that the non-penetrative, pain-free sexual acts of the parents were not distinguishable by the children from the carrying, hugging, kissing, stroking, and soothing that are a huge and necessary element of all normal parenting.[49] Children have no way to know what constitutes permissible or "normal" touching other than by what is

---

49. See the seminal study of René Spitz captured in a documentary film: *Grief: A Peril in Infancy*, Films Media Group. Accessed March 6, 2018. The studies that René Spitz conducted in the 1940s were the first to show more systematically that social interactions with other humans are essential for children's development. Spitz followed two groups of children from the time they were born until they were several years old. The children in the first group were raised in an orphanage, where the babies received only minimal human contact in their cribs, because a single nurse had to care for seven children. The children in the second group of babies were raised in a nursery in a prison where their mothers were incarcerated. These mothers were allowed to give their babies unlimited care and affection every day, and the babies were able to see one another and the prison staff throughout the day.

presented to them at home, and one of the principles of the Doe family secret society was for the children to never ask other children what went on in their homes. As their father/ step-grandfather phrased it to them, "Other families have their private ways also."

Before we go further, I want to stress that the sexualized touching of Seth and Ashley by their family members *in a framework where there was no other type of physical or psychological abuse whatsoever* was entirely a one-off case. In the hundreds of childhood sexual abuse cases I became familiar with in three decades of legal representation of children's social service agencies, I never saw a second case where sexual abuse was imposed upon children in isolation from other concomitant stressors, typically including physical and psychological abuse.[50]

The situation in the Doe household was a quintessential case of a dangerous *connection*. The Doe children had been made fully aware of the *danger* involved if they disclosed the family incest outside the house, but instead of using the fear

---

At age four months, the state of development of the two groups of babies was similar: the babies in the orphanage even scored a higher average on certain tests. But by the time the babies were one-year-olds, the motor and intellectual performance of those reared in the orphanage lagged badly behind those reared in the prison nursery. The orphanage babies were also less curious, less playful, and more subject to infections. During their second and third years of life, the children being raised by their mothers in prison walked and talked confidently and showed development comparable to that of children raised in normal family settings. But of the twenty-six children reared in the orphanage, only two could walk and manage a few words. Since the time of Spitz's pioneering study, many other experiments have shown the catastrophic effects sensory and social deprivation have on children's subsequent development.

50. Please see the Appendix to this paper, which provides a remarkably well-done summary of the literature on the seriously deleterious effects of childhood sexual abuse on its victims. The summary was authored by Ms. Christie Kim of the Department of Applied Psychology, New York University Steinhardt, and is reprinted with her permission.

of separation to motivate the children, the family had managed to emphasize the *connective* aspects of the family secret society to prompt their compliance. For these two children, we know that the connection factor greatly outweighed the danger factor, because absent Ashley's finding and playing "inappropriately" with the anatomically correct dolls in her mother's social worker's office, both children might well have grown to adulthood without any disclosure from the inside or any discovery from the outside. Dr. Putnam and I spent hours trying to speculate about what would have become of these children if the accidental disclosure had never occurred. Would they have exhibited exaggerated sexuality with other children when they reached puberty? Would they have become angry with their parents once they came to understand the extreme deviancy of the family incest? How would their own sexuality have played out in their adult relationships?

*

What we did learn with certainty about the two children was that their incestuous behavior did not end with the accidental disclosure of the sexuality in their birth home and their immediate removal. After half a year in two different emergency foster homes, the children were placed separately in two subsequent long-term foster homes.[51] After about a year in the second set of foster homes, the siblings were placed together by an adoption agency (my client, hence my involvement) in what seemed to be an ideal pre-adoptive home. The details of what transpired in the adoptive home are set forth in "The Loneliest Boy," so here I will only supply a bare-bones summary of what

---

51. It is interesting to note that we deposed all four sets of the very experienced foster parents who had been chosen by the Department of Social Services to care for the siblings, and all eight deponents testified that neither Seth nor Ashley exhibited any sexualization whatsoever in dealing with other children in the four different foster homes.

we learned: eighteen months into the placement, the adoptive parents discovered that the siblings had a secret sex life with each other. Several times a week, in the middle of the night when the adoptive parents were fast asleep, one sibling would tiptoe down the hallway into the other's bedroom, and they would cuddle up in bed together, sometimes just hugging and giggling together, sometimes touching each other sexually. And sometimes they would have intercourse, or such intercourse as prepubic, latency-age children can have.

The information Dr. Putnam garnered in his examinations of the two children, combined with what we attorneys gathered from our depositions of the siblings, brought us to the conclusion that, for these children, these secret encounters were more ritual than sexual. We became convinced that these prepubescent children weren't really having sex, and that they also weren't involved in childish exploratory sex play. Something entirely different was going on here. Something entirely unique. These children, we concluded, were *connecting*—connecting with each other as they had been socialized to do—and connecting through their sexualized acts with their somatically stored memories of what it *felt like* to be part of the birth family they missed and pined for. This was, obviously, not a societally acceptable mode of connection—quite the contrary—but for these two children, it was connection nonetheless.

*

While Seth and Ashley had no way of assessing the deviance and criminality of the incest they experienced in their birth home, we know that this was no longer the case with respect to their inter-sibling incest in the pre-adoptive home. By this time, they had seen firsthand society's swift and certain reaction to incest: every adult member of their family had almost immediately pled guilty to multiple felonies. When I examined the children in their depositions to learn if they understood exactly *why* they had lost their birth family, they testified that they had understood perfectly well. In other words, they acknowledged that in their pre-adoptive home, they knew—and discussed—that if they were ever caught in their inter-sibling incest, they would likely lose their adoptive family with all its advantages. So, the key question became: Why would these bright and intact children expose themselves to a charge of incest—one of society's most deviant and swiftly punished acts—when they knew how abrupt and inevitable the reaction would be if they were ever caught?

To us, the answer became clear, if complex. Seth and Ashley knew no other mode of connecting with each other— or at least none that could offer the depth of connection they experienced in their sexualized touching. The two siblings, of course, knew other modes of connecting with each other: they played normal children's games with one another, they walked to school together, and so on. But these routine interactions were like swimming in the shallow end of a pool—you can only go so deep. When they added touch, the pool deepened. And when the touch became sexualized, they were back in the deep end of the pool—where they had been taught to swim.

In other words, the sexualized touching was used by the children to reestablish an emotional connection back to their family, back to the life they had known and now missed. Dr. Putnam and I speculated whether the drive to reconnect with their birth family would have been less controlling on their future behavior if their transition from their birth home had been handled differently. Remember, these children were removed the very evening of the accidental discovery of their birth-family incest, and never—*ever*—did they see anyone in their family again. We came to the conclusion that, from a psychiatric point of view, the court had erred greatly when it immediately accepted felony plea bargains from the parents and sent them out of state *with no involvement of the children whatsoever in any formal courtroom proceedings.* We thought that the children might well have been better off psychiatrically if they had experienced their parents suffering through a full criminal trial. There might have been closure had the children seen their parents arriving at the courtroom in handcuffs, being convicted of their crimes, and then being sentenced by the court to long-term imprisonment. Psychiatrically, we felt, the children needed a ritual break with their family: if that had occurred, they might have been better able to purge themselves of the incestuous subculture that had been instilled in them in the birth-family household. They needed the equivalent of what funeral services provide: public acknowledgment and emotional processing of the loss of a loved one. Arguably, Dr. Putnam and I thought, the absence of their involvement in a judicial public ritual had cost them dearly.

Scores of readers have asked me over the several years since the publication of "The Loneliest Boy" if I ever learned anything more about Seth's fate after he disappeared from his halfway house just days before his eighteenth birthday. The answer is no—but with one exception. One day, in a courthouse hallway, I ran into the court-appointed attorney who had served as Seth's guardian ad litem during the litigation and who had subsequently served as the trustee of the trust that had been settled in Seth's favor to hold his part of the settlement funds from the litigation. I learned that Seth had never shown up to claim his money—and this was the better part of a decade after the litigation. Not a promising sign.

*

The misconnection between Seth and Ashley Doe was in some ways the most dangerous misconnection case I ever encountered. But over the years, quite a few other cases brought me into contact with clients whose closest connections brought them more pain than pleasure. Healthy connections provide each of us with sanctuary—with safety and support and soothing—and sometimes, even with love. Dangerous misconnections, in contrast, expose one (and sometimes both) participants to a life full of terror and dread. In one such law case, I represented a twenty-two-year-old woman who had suffered nearly four years of entrapment in a cult; she had been disallowed both physically and psychologically from leaving the remote compound where the cult leader ruled with absolute power, doing whatever he wanted, whenever he wanted, with whomever he wanted. During this period, she was entirely cut off from everyone she had ever known, most particularly from her parents and siblings. Her description of the domination of the cult leader over her and her fellow cult members sounded more authoritarian, more sexualized, and more bizarre than Hollywood would dare to paint. Finally entrusted by the cult leader to go on a procurement expedition to the local town—amazingly and admirably—my client had garnered the strength to call her parents and arrange an escape. But even after she returned to the safety of her parents' home, her dangerous misconnection did not end so easily: she began receiving frightening threats leveled at her family if she did not return. Her parents retained my services, and my task was to negotiate peace terms with her eccentric and sadistic— if enigmatically charismatic—cult leader. I can assure you, this was one of the more bizarre and unusual negotiations of my legal career.

Dangerous misconnections abounded in the pedophilia scandal that has rocked the Catholic Church internationally, but began in Boston. Given that a goodly number of my clients were psychiatrists, many of whom specialized in trauma psychiatry, on a number of occasions they referred adult patients to me who had recovered or unmasked buried memories of their childhood sexual abuse by priests and other Church-linked individuals. The stories I heard were casebook examples of dangerous connections, precisely because the families of the abused boys were so inextricably connected to their church, that they could not permit themselves to listen to, let alone act on, their own children's reports of being groomed or abused. Suing the Catholic Church on behalf of these victims was a David and Goliath situation, and hence a legal undertaking that took enormous resources and specialized focus. There were several attorneys in Boston who became specialists in this undertaking, and it was to them that I referred all such cases.

One of the most skillful and daring among them was an attorney named Eric MacLeish, who had become quite well known in this time frame for his two-week-long deposition of Cardinal Bernard Law. MacLeish's efforts were instrumental in the process leading to the cardinal's resignation and inter-national ignominy and, more importantly, to the disclosure of thousands of documents that proved beyond a shadow of a doubt that the Church had had detailed information for decades about hundreds of abusive priests—and done noth-ing about it. MacLeish and his team won a huge settlement for more than five hundred clients, and assured himself of a stream of referrals from attorneys like me when we learned of new cases. But this brilliant young attorney was destined to go through his own personal hell: his legal services to sexual abuse victims awakened in him his own repressed memories of having been abused at summer camp by a Church-linked scoutmaster. At this discovery, MacLeish developed extremely severe post-traumatic stress disorder and required long-term clinical therapy. Incredibly—even ironically—MacLeish and his female clinician developed a dangerous misconnection of their own, with the therapist later being stripped of her license for entering into a sexual relationship with MacLeish.

Dangerous misconnections are often tragic connections—in the formal Greek tragedy sense of the term—for they bear within themselves the seeds of their own explosive destruction. At some point—no doubt not always, but often—the dangerous element overcomes the cohesive element, and the connection is blown asunder. MacLeish lost his marriage over the affair with his therapist and was compelled by his declining emotional health to give up the practice of law for the calm of academia. The cult leader in the case I mentioned above was arrested on multiple felony charges two years after I negotiated my client's release from his clutches.[52] And the Doe children, if they are both still alive, will never see each other again—after having previously lost every single other blood relative in their family. Dangerous misconnections can be—tend to be—devastatingly unstable.

Conclusion

At the outset of this essay, I presented to you a list of "modes of misconnection" that set forth the five genres of misconnection that plagued the lives of the children I met whose

---

52. The ultimate, Greek-tragedy-level example of how the defective connection that lies at the very heart of a cult is doomed to end with tragedy is that of Jim Jones. Jones had taken his Disciples of Christ cult first to California and later to Guyana. In 1978, US Representative Leo Ryan took a congressional delegation to Guyana both to investigate reports that the cult was holding adherents against their will and to offer a means of immediate escape for those who so chose. Ryan, his delegation, and those few cult members who indeed chose to leave were all gunned down, followed by Jones initiating a mass murder-suicide of over nine hundred persons—over three hundred of whom were children—almost all of whom died by drinking cyanide-laced Kool-Aid. Parents fed their children poisoned Kool-Aid; that is a dangerous connection I simply cannot get my arms around.

circumstances were significantly impacted by the malfunctioning of their relationship with their parents. Of course many of these children presented with other psychological and behavioral issues as well, but all of them were significantly misconnected with their parents in one way or another. You, my reader, can judge for yourself if you found this analytical model helpful in understanding the cases presented above under each category of misconnection. But in asking myself whether or not there is any significant explanatory power to be derived from employing the model, I came upon the idea of looking at the *inverse* of the suggested descriptive modes of misconnections to see if the inverted model did a decent job of describing the functioning of *healthy parent-child relationships*. Here is how that exercise came out:

Parent-Child Bonds:
Misconnections Contrasted with Healthy Connections

- Obstructed Connection *versus* Unobstructed Connection
- One-Way Connection *versus* A Connection That Is Rewarding for Both Parties
- Fraudulent Connection *versus* Honest and Full Communication
- Tenuous Connection *versus* Assured and Certain Connection
- Dangerous Connection *versus* A Safe and Nurturing Connection

Perhaps the most immediate method to test out if the "healthy connection" side of the ledger is useful is to ask you, my reader, to bring up in your mind your very closest friendship. When I perform the same exercise, I find that it checks out right down the list. Close friends find time for each other, no matter how busy their lives are; they both find the relationship rewarding; when they speak, they are open and frank with each other; they both cherish the relationship and look forward to carrying it on indefinitely; and, finally, they are gentle with each other so that each feels safe and nurtured.

Now, permit me to apply this logic of looking at the healthy connections side of the ledger to the topic of parenting, and the parent-child relationship:

Unobstructed Connection. Clearly, part of successful parenting is taking the time to do so. I, for one, was guilty of allowing a fledgling law career to keep me away from far too many Little League baseball games. Once my wife succeeded in getting this across to me, a few clients waited a little longer for a resolution of their matters, but I got to see a line-drive home run hook over the left field fence and the smile that spread across my son's face when the coach later gave him the "game ball." By the way, another Little League game took place when my father was visiting from out of state. In that game, my boy was honored with another "game ball," and after the game he signed the ball in his childish scrawl and presented it to my dad as a gift. That ball spent the rest of my father's life on his coffee table. How much does that have to say about the power of intergenerational family connections?

Rewarding for Both Parties. Human children are dependent on and attached to their parents for an extremely long period of time compared to other mammals. And, from the other side, successful parents love being parents, in the way gardeners take delight in the flowers and fruits they raise with their hard work. When parent-child relationships are rewarding for both parties, everybody wins. And while this seems abstractly true in our era of nuclear families, it would have seemed all

the more an accurate description of everyday life in the multigenerational families that characterized traditional community life around the globe until so very recently. The personal
finances of many atomic families of our times are crushed by
massive expenses for day care for their children and elder care
for their parents—recent inventions that were unnecessary,
and probably even inconceivable, when grandparents took loving care of their grandchildren and mothers worked at home. It
could be that the principal obstruction of our times that leads
to parent-child misconnection is the structure of our economy
itself. That's not good news.

Honest and Full Communication. Arguably, children watch
what you do more than they listen to what you say; but what
you say is still terribly important. Patiently answering all those
"why" questions doesn't just inform a small child about how
the world works: it tells them how *you* work. Verbal communications between a parent and child have two levels, the way
Asian script writing can simultaneously convey a meaning and
be a form of visual art. A parent's tone of voice can be loving
and nurturing, even when the content of their speech is disci-
plining and corrective. The French sociology professor under
whom I wrote my doctoral dissertation told me that his father,
a doctor and a leading member of the prestigious Académie
Nationale de Médecine in Paris, never once told him "I love
you," nor, for that matter, did he ever speak to his son in a gentle, nurturing voice. When later I became a professor and was
able to invite my ex-professor to give a monthlong summer
seminar at Boston University, I watched him do exactly the
opposite with his two children, purposefully raising them with
all the physical warmth and verbal expressions of love typical of today's parenting style. One of those children is today a
respected medical doctor and professor of medicine, while the
other was recently France's minister of social affairs and health,

and she now sits on the Conseil d'État, a branch of France's supreme court. Pretty good job of parenting there—and it was all about substituting open and loving communication for the formal and emotion-free communication of another era.

Assured and Certain Connections. Children cherish continuity in every aspect of their lives. Their room, their toys, their pals, their home, their neighborhood: from their point of view, nothing should ever change. And this inherent comfort with the status quo, this aversion to change and uncertainty, this comfort in familiarity, is magnified a thousandfold when it comes to children's preferences with regard to their parents. In several cases where I had the opportunity to confer with adopted older children whose socioeconomic status had increased monumentally between their birth home and their adoptive home—not a single one thought that was a good thing. I also had numerous conversations with "parentified" children who, before the social service authorities had surmised what was happening and intervened, had taken on the awesome responsibility of caring for their incompetent, drug-addled, or alcoholic parent. Generally, if these children's life circumstances were anywhere near tolerable, their preference would have been to opt for the status quo so as not to be removed from their birth parents. We often had to work hard to convince such children of the necessity of moving on, particularly if they didn't perceive a palpable absence of safety.

Safe and Nurturing Connection. This was the category where my personal experiences with my child and nieces/nephews—and my observations of my friends' children—varied most extremely from my professional experiences with children from compromised families. I don't imagine fish spend a lot of time thinking about water—it's just there. Similarly, children born to families that treasure them and have adequate

resources to raise them don't seem to spend any time thinking about safety and certainty—it's just there. But children
from failing families, children with compromised parents who
lack the psychological or socio-financial capacity to take care
of their offspring, live with a level of anxiety and uncertainty
that can be positively devastating. During my career, I had
dozens of conversations during termination-of-parental-rights
litigation with children who still loved their parents but who
reluctantly admitted to us—and more importantly to themselves—that they had come to understand that their parents
could not keep them safe. It doesn't get any sadder than that.

*

Looking at all five inverted categories together, it seems safe
to say that when a parent-child relationship is unobstructed
by too much distraction, when it is experienced as mutually
rewarding, when it is full of lovingly intoned honest communication, and when it is unquestionably permanent and per-
sistently nurturing—then we are looking at a fully healthy
environment in which a child can develop the neural pathways
that will equip the child to successfully connect with others as
they move progressively out of their home and into the world.

The reasonably robust explanatory power the model has
provided on the healthy-relationship side of the ledger argues
for the usefulness of the "misconnection" categories I have
proposed on the not-so-healthy side of the ledger. My hope
is that the mode-of-misconnection analysis I am proposing
might prove helpful in analyzing in what precise way(s) a deficient parent-child relationship is malfunctioning and thereby
help family-counseling therapists intervene effectively. A rig-
orous test of what I am proposing, in other words, will depend
on whether or not family-counseling and related mental
health professionals find that the model provides them useful

diagnostic and treatment insights in their active clinical settings. Several mental health professionals with whom I have worked over the years are currently taking a look at the utility of the model in their clinical work with children and families, and I look forward to hearing and reporting on their feedback in the near future.

APPENDIX[53]

A Review of the Literature on the Effects on Children of Childhood Sexual Abuse

CHRISTIE KIM, NEW YORK UNIVERSITY

Studies conducted across decades of research have established that between 9 to 30 percent of children in North America experience sexual abuse (Briere and Elliott, 2003; Glaser, 2013; Finkelhor, 1994). With regard to gender, approximately 20 to 30 percent of girls and 5 to 10 percent of boys experience sexual abuse at least once during childhood (Briere and Elliott, 2003; Finkelhor, 1994). Child sexual abuse (CSA) is understood to be the engagement in any sexual behavior with a child under the age of eighteen who is unable to comprehend or give consent to a sexual act due to one's age or developmental stage (Finkelhor and Browne, 1985). Forms of sexual abuse include violation of the body by use of force, coercion, or against the will of the child, as well as exposure to sexual media (Finkelhor and Browne, 1985; Foster and Hagedorn, 2014). The traumatic experience of sexual abuse, particularly in childhood and adolescence, is associated with low self-efficacy, defined as the belief in one's own ability to effectively function and exercise control within a situation (Bandura, 1982; Benight and Bandura, 2004; Finkelhor and Browne, 1985; Lamoureux, Palmieri, Jackson, and Hobfoll, 2011). Self-efficacy diminishes due to CSA, as victims experience significant decreases in self-esteem, mastery, and agency following the abuse (Cecil and Matson, 2001; Cieslak, Benight, and Caden Lehman, 2008; Foster and Hagedorn, 2014; Finkelhor and Browne, 1985; Hagan and Smail, 1997; Lamoureux et al., 2011).

Researchers suggest that victims' lowered sense of self-efficacy largely mediates the relation between CSA and disruptions in a child's emotional, cognitive, and interpersonal development (Benight and Bandura, 2004; Finkelhor and Browne, 1985; Lamoureux et al., 2011). In particular, self-efficacy predicts the amount of effort a child is able to put forth in persevering through adverse experiences such as CSA, as well as levels of vulnerability to stress and mental illness, self-motivation, resilience, and the nature of the victim's decision-making and outlook on life (Bandura, 1982; Benight and Bandura, 2004; Cieslak et al., 2008). Decreased self-efficacy due to CSA also increases the risk for negative mental health and behavioral outcomes such as post-traumatic stress disorder (PTSD), including symptoms of disassociation, re-victimization, self-devaluation, and maladaptive coping mechanisms, such as self-harm and suicidal ideation (Bagley, Berlitho, and Bertrand, 1995; Benight and Bandura, 2004; Cieslak et al., 2008; Coohey, 2010; Lamoureux et al., 2011; Lev-Wiesel, 2000; Reese-Weber and Smith, 2011; Stern, Lynch, Oates, O'Toole, and Cooney, 1995). However, these detrimental effects do not develop in all victims of CSA, and the intensity and duration of symptoms vary between individuals

(Briere and Elliott, 2003). Still, research suggests that the level of self-efficacy may be predictive of the recovery period for victims. More specifically, self-efficacy is thought to influence important steps of recovery, such as help-seeking behavior, resource utilization, disclosure of abuse, and reporting the offense (Finkelhor and Browne, 1985; Foster and Hagedorn, 2014; Lev-Wiesel, 2000).

There is a multitude of empirical studies that provide support for the relation between CSA and negative psychosocial outcomes, yet few studies focus particularly on the outcomes associated with decreased self-efficacy. Accordingly, the present review seeks to explore how lowered self-efficacy due to child sexual abuse predicts disruption in victims' affective, cognitive, and interpersonal development.

Negative Affect

Fear and anxiety. The traumatic experience of CSA is detrimental to the emotional state of victims both during and long after the offense (Foster and Hagedorn, 2014). Fear has been identified as the predominant emotion in young victims during experiences of CSA. Descriptive firsthand accounts indicate that children feel a deep sense of helplessness and powerlessness during sexual abuse (Foster and Hagedorn, 2014). Furthermore, fear of the repercussions following disclosing the abuse (e.g., parental rejection or skepticism) was found to predict both a lack of or a delayed disclosure (Foster and Hagedorn, 2014). Negative emotional states in victims of CSA further contribute to anxiety. Compared to those without a history of abuse, CSA is correlated with significantly higher levels of anxiety, including anxious arousal and anxiety disorders, across the lifetime (Bagley et al., 1995; Briere and Elliott, 2003; Swanston et al., 2003). Lowered self-efficacy due to CSA predicts negative affect, such as fear and anxiety, in victims in both the immediate and delayed aftermath.

Depression and self-blame. The negative emotional experiences of CSA victims are further apparent through increased levels of depression and self-blame. Following fear, feelings of sadness, inefficacy, worthlessness, and shame were found to be prevalent throughout children's experiences of CSA (Foster and Hagedorn, 2014). A large number of studies have found that CSA predicts higher rates of self-reported sadness and depression across age groups, as well as despair and hopelessness in young individuals exposed to sexual abuse, as compared to those who did not experience sexual abuse (Bagley et al., 1995; Briere and Elliott, 2003; Cecil and Matson, 2001; Lamoureux et al., 2011; Stern et al., 1995; Swanston, et al., 2003). Along with symptoms of depression, victims of CSA often develop internalizing symptoms such as self-blame (Foster and Hagedorn, 2014; Hagan and Smail, 1997). For example, Cieslak et al. (2008) found that CSA predicts decreased coping self-efficacy, defined as the belief in one's efficaciousness, particularly in mastering the demands of post-abuse recovery, which then predicted blaming oneself for the abuse. Another study found that, among adults who experienced CSA, roughly half of both male and female victims turned the blame inward and attributed the fault of the abuse to themselves (Lev-Wiesel, 2000). The perception that the abuse occurred because of a personal inability to prevent it reflects the diminished sense of self-efficacy following CSA.

Self-harm and suicidality. Lowered self-efficacy due to CSA is characterized by a decreased sense of agency, which has been found to be significantly predictive of externalizing mental health symptoms, specifically, self-harm and suicidality (Bagley et al., 1995; Briere and Elliott, 2003; O'Connor, Rasmussen, and Hawton, 2009). Compared to non-abused individuals, adolescent victims of CSA report significantly more frequent self-harm and suicidal behaviors (Bagley et al., 1995), a relation that is particularly strong in girls (Noll, Horowitz, Bonanno, Trickett, and Putnam, 2008). The high frequency of externalizing symptoms among victims of CSA reflects disruption in affect regulation due to low self-efficacy.

Disruptions in Cognitions

Self-esteem. Decreased self-efficacy has been linked with disruptions in cognitive development in child victims of sexual abuse. Self-esteem is a crucial component of self-efficacy, as it reflects the valuation of self-worth, and it is often impaired in victims of CSA (Finkelhor and Browne, 1985; Hagan and Smail, 1997). Multiple studies have found that children, adolescents, and young adults who experienced sexual abuse during childhood tend to have significantly lower levels of self-esteem and self-worth than their peers who had no such history (Cecil and Matson, 2001; Larmoureaux et al., 2011; Stern et al., 1995; Swanston et al., 2003). Negative cognitions about the self, including self-blame, self-hatred, guilt, and feeling damaged, are indicative of the depreciated senses of self-esteem as a result of lowered self-efficacy in the aftermath of sexual abuse (Hagan and Smail, 1997; Lev-Wiesel, 2000; Noll et al., 2003; Reese-Weber and Smith, 2011).

Mastery and agency. Decreased self-efficacy as the result of force or coercion during a sexual assault can severely damage a child's cognitive sense of mastery and agency. Mastery, the belief in personal control over life circumstances, and agency, the perceived capability of self-determination, are significantly lower in victims of CSA (Bandura, 1982; Bandura, Reese, and

Adams, 1982; Benight and Bandura, 2004; Finkelhor and Browne, 1985). Self-efficacy is contravened when the abuser exerts total power over the victim, instilling a sense of powerlessness through manipulation, secrecy, and threats of punishment (Finkelhor and Browne, 1985; Hagan and Smail, 1997). Research has found that in comparison to those who did not experience CSA, adolescent females with a history of CSA reported a decreased sense of mastery and control in their lives (Benight and Bandura, 2004; Cecil and Matson, 2001). Lower levels of coping self-efficacy, in particular, reflected women's diminished belief in their ability to master adaptive skills in the period following the trauma (Cieslak et al., 2008). The overwhelming sense of perceived inability to control life situations is intricately related to further cognitive disruptions in CSA victims.

Dissociation. Across both gender and age groups, those with a history of CSA often exhibit dissociative cognitions as a result of impaired self-efficacy. Habitual dissociation was found in a CSA case study by Hagan and Smail (1997), in which a young female victim mentally disconnected from her body as she felt powerless to escape the pain and feared her resistance would yield punishment. Adult men and women who experienced CSA exhibited higher scores of dissociation compared to those who were not abused (Briere and Elliott, 2003). For women specifically, an earlier age of onset of CSA was significantly related to higher dissociative scores (Groth-Marnat and Michel, 2000). The psychological trauma of CSA predicts a decreased sense of efficaciousness, resulting in a significant increase in dissociative cognition.

The self and body. Lowered self-efficacy is predictive of dysfunctional eating behaviors, most notably those which are linked to dissociation. Mercado, Martínez-Taboas, and Pedrosa

(2008) found that females with a history of CSA scored significantly higher on a measure of dysfunctional eating-related cognitions, such as bulimia nervosa, and the related behaviors of bingeing and self-induced vomiting (Swanston et al., 2003). Furthermore, both a history of CSA and the disordered eating were found to be highly correlated with dissociative experiences, as extreme eating serves as a medium for escaping unpleasant or painful feelings (Groth-Marnat and Michel, 2000; Mercado et al., 2008). A loss of control and derealization following CSA are reflected in dysfunctional bulimic behaviors, which include severely restricted eating intake, purging, use of laxatives or diuretics, and extreme exercise (Groth-Marnat and Michel, 2000; Mercado et al., 2008). These disordered cognitions and related behaviors are symptomatic of a traumatic loss of control and agency.

The Interpersonal Context of Child Sexual Abuse

Interpersonal relationships. A history of CSA has been found to predict interpersonal adversity due to decreased effectiveness in relationships. For instance, women who were sexually abused during childhood display significantly less effective interpersonal skills (Kearns and Calhoun, 2014). Research shows that young males and females who report experiences of CSA were more likely to fight with family members, have poor relationships with their mothers, and see their friendships end, compared to those who did not experience abuse (Stern et al., 1995; Swanston et al., 2003). Similarly, Lamoureux et al. (2011) found that, over time, young female victims of CSA tended to exhibit higher levels of psychological distress and social conflict than non-victims. These young women subsequently reported interpersonal resource loss and greater deficiency in social support (Lamoureux et al., 2011). These findings suggest that low self-efficacy due to CSA has a disruptive influence on the development of interpersonal skills, such as regulating and resolving conflict, reaching compromise, or persisting in long-term relationships (Kearns and Calhoun, 2014; Lamoureux et al., 2011; Stern et al., 1995; Swanston et al., 2003).

Sexual self-efficacy. The disruptive impact of lowered self-efficacy on interpersonal relationships is pervasive throughout victims' romantic and sexual interactions, as a strong negative relation between sexual abuse in childhood and self-efficacy has been found across numerous studies (Coohey, 2010; Hovsepian et al., 2010; Noll et al., 2003). Female victims of CSA tend to have lower levels of sexual self-efficacy in comparison to those who did not experience sexual abuse (Kearns and Calhoun, 2014). As a result, research shows that men and women who experience CSA reported having greater concerns regarding sexual interactions, such as sexual distress, dissatisfaction, or unwanted thoughts about sex (Briere and Elliott, 2003). The threat of CSA on victims' self-efficacy is linked to deficits in control pertaining to sexual relations; diminished sexual self-efficacy, in turn, predicts victims' ability to voice their desires.

Decreased belief in one's ability to be effective, especially in regards to sexual relationships, appears to silence the voices of childhood victims. Specifically, adolescent girls who were sexually abused report feeling less able to communicate about their sexuality with their partner (Hovsepian et al., 2010). In addition, women do not always feel capable of either giving or denying genuine consent. These women presented higher sexual permissiveness, which Noll et al. (2003) believes may unintentionally communicate a willingness to engage in a sexual act despite insufficient emotional and sexual maturity. Furthermore, women with multiple experiences of sexual abuse were more likely to report decreased sexual assertiveness skills

(Kearns and Calhoun, 2014). The experience of CSA is detrimental to victims' perceived ability to be efficacious within interpersonal interactions, which puts victims at greater risk for future offenses and risky sex practices.

Safe sex practices. Decreased efficacy following CSA also impacts victims' safe sex practices and can increase risky sexual behaviors. Adolescent girls in particular report feeling less able to communicate about the method and frequency of their contraception use (Hovsepian et al., 2010). Lamoureux et al. (2011) also found that the experience of CSA for females had a significantly negative effect on self-efficacy, which further predicted HIV and sexually risky behaviors. Additional research indicates that the decreased sense of self-efficacy leads to a lack of confidence in negotiating safe sex. Specifically, victims reported higher fears of condom negotiation and were significantly less likely to use condoms on a consistent basis (Brown et al., 2014; Lamoureux et al., 2011). These findings also revealed weaker levels of power in victims' sexual relationships with men, and decreased self-efficacy in refusing unwanted sexual activity (Brown et al., 2014).

Re-victimization. Decreased self-efficacy further predicts subsequent re-victimization as victims of CSA may feel incapable of protecting themselves against future unwanted advances or assaults (Finkelhor and Browne, 1985; Reese-Weber and Smith, 2011). Multiple studies have found that both men and women are more than twice as likely to experience both sexual and physical victimization if they have experienced sexual abuse in childhood (Noll et al., 2003; Reese-Weber and Smith, 2011; Swanston et al., 2003). In women specifically, decreased self-efficacy due to CSA was found to have a causal effect in increasing the likelihood of sexual victimization (Kearns and Calhoun, 2010). These findings suggest that decreased self-efficacy predicted by CSA leads to diminished efficacy and dissociative tendencies in risky interpersonal situations.

Conclusion

This exploration of the impact of sexual abuse illuminates the role of perceived self-efficacy in the well-being of those who were victimized in childhood, with particular emphasis on disruptive effects on victims' affect, cognitions, and interpersonal relationships. Decreased sense of self-efficacy due to CSA was found to predict negative affect, which was associated with increased rates of self-harm and suicidality (Bagley et al., 1995; Briere and Elliott, 2003; Swanston et al., 2003). Victims of CSA experienced disruptive cognitions as well, such as dissociation and related behavioral disorders (Benight and Bandura, 2004; Cecil and Matson, 2001; Cieslak et al., 2008; Swanston et al., 2003). Furthermore, individuals with a history of CSA were found to have ineffective interpersonal skills, which led to greater conflict, risky sexual behaviors and re-victimization (Hovsepian et al., 2010; Kearns and Calhoun, 2010; Lamoureux et al., 2011; Swanston et al., 2003).

Across the studies included in this review, a primary limitation inherent to the subject of CSA is the discrepancy between actual and reported cases of CSA (Finkelhor, 1994). Similarly, while most of the studies operationalized CSA in the same way that it was presented in this review, there remains variation in the exact definition and examples of CSA throughout the literature. Furthermore, the generally limited amount of research focusing explicitly on the construct of self-efficacy called for the inclusion of studies that referenced more narrowed components, such as affect, self-esteem, mastery, and agency, which may imply relations that were not explicitly measured (Bandura, 1982; Benight and Bandura, 2004; Coohey, 2010;

Finkelhor and Browne, 1985). In the future, studies should focus specifically on self-efficacy as a dynamic construct, to develop a clear model of the influence of CSA on self-efficacy, understand how self-efficacy disrupts key developmental components that are crucial for recovery, and identify potential risk and protective factors. Finally, male participants were largely underrepresented throughout the literature; therefore, many findings, specifically those regarding interpersonal relationships, may not be generalizable beyond female victims of CSA.

In addition to the emotional implications of such abuse, the strength of perceived self-efficacy may be predictive of victims' help-seeking, resource utilization, and likelihood of reporting abuse (Finkelhor and Browne, 1985; Foster and Hagedorn, 2014; Lev-Wiesel, 2000). With the understanding that self-efficacy can be developed over time, this review stresses the importance of appropriate therapeutic treatment and interventions for victims of sexual violence (Bandura, 1982; Bandura et al., 1982; Kearns and Calhoun, 2010). Future research should aim to gather samples of greater diversity specifically in gender, race, and culture, and explore the effects of self-efficacy interventions and treatment on victims' recovery.

REFERENCES TO THE APPENDIX

Bagley, Christopher, Floyd Bolitho, and Lorne Bertrand. "Mental Health Profiles, Suicidal Behavior, and Community Sexual Assault in 2112 Canadian Adolescents." *Crisis: The Journal of Crisis Intervention and Suicide Prevention* 16, no. 3 (1995): 126–31, https://doi.org/10.1027/0227-5910.16.3.126.

Bandura, Albert. "Self-Efficacy Mechanism in Human Agency." *American Psychologist* 37, no. 2 (1982): 122–47, https://doi.org/10.1037/0003-066X.37.2.122.

Benight, Charles C., and Albert Bandura. "Social Cognitive Theory of Posttraumatic Recovery: The Role of Perceived Self-Efficacy." *Behaviour Research and Therapy* 42, no. 10 (2004): 1129–48, https://doi.org/10.1016/j.brat.2003.08.008.

Briere, John, and Diana M. Elliott. "Prevalence and Psychological Sequelae of Self-Reported Childhood Physical and Sexual Abuse in a General Population Sample of Men and Women." *Child Abuse and Neglect* 27, no. 10 (2003): 1205–22, https://doi.org/10.1016/j.chiabu.2003.09.008.

Brown, Jennifer L., April M. Young, Jessica M. Sales, Ralph J. DiClemente, Eve S. Rose, and Gina M. Wingood. "Impact of Abuse History on Adolescent African American Women's Current HIV/STD-Associated Behaviors and Psychosocial Mediators of HIV/STD Risk." *Journal of Aggression, Maltreatment & Trauma* 23, no. 2 (2014): 151–67, https://doi.org/10.1080/10926771.2014.873511.

Cecil, Heather, and Steven C. Matson. "Psychological Functioning and Family Discord among African-American Adolescent Females with and without a History of Childhood Sexual Abuse." *Child Abuse & Neglect* 25, no. 7 (2001): 973–88, https://doi.org/10.1016/S0145-2134(01)00250-2.

Cieslak, Roman, Charles C. Benight, and Victoria Caden Lehman. "Coping Self-Efficacy Mediates the Effects of Negative Cognitions on Posttraumatic Distress." *Behaviour Research and Therapy* 46, no. 7 (2008): 788–98, https://doi.org/10.1016/j.brat.2008.03.007.

Coohey, Carol. "Gender Differences in Internalizing Problems among Sexually Abused Early Adolescents." *Child Abuse & Neglect* 34, no. 11 (2010): 856–62, https://doi.org/10.1016/j.chiabu.2010.05.001.

Finkelhor, David. "Current Information on the Scope and Nature of Child Sexual Abuse." *The Future of Children* 4, no. 2 (1994): 31–53, https://doi.org/10.2307/1602522.

Finkelhor, David, and Angela Browne. "The Traumatic Impact of Child Sexual Abuse: A Conceptualization." *American Journal of Orthopsychiatry* 55, no. 4 (1985): 530–41, https://doi.org/10.1111/j.1939-0025.1985.tb02703.x.

Foster, Jennifer M., and W. Bryce Hagedorn. "Through the Eyes of the Wounded: A Narrative Analysis of Children's Sexual Abuse Experiences and Recovery Process." *Journal of Child Sexual Abuse* 23, no. 5 (2014): 538–57, https://doi .org/10.1080/10538712.2014.918072.

Glaser, Danya. "Child Maltreatment." *Psychiatry* 7, no. 7 (2008): 295–8, http://doi.org/10.1016.j.mppsy.2008.05.001.

Groth-Marnat, Gary, and Naomi Michel. "Dissociation, Comorbidity of Dissociative Disorders, and Childhood Abuse in a Community Sample of Women with Current and Past Bulimia." *Social Behavior and Personality: An International Journal* 28, no. 3 (2000): 279–92, https://doi .org/10.2224/sbp.2000.28.3.279.

Hagan, Teresa, and David Smail. "Power-Mapping—II. Practical Application: The Example of Child Sexual Abuse." *Journal of Community & Applied Social Psychology* 7, no. 4 (1997): 269–84, https://doi.org/10.1002/(SICI)1099-1298(199709)7:4<269::AID-CASP429>3.0.CO;2-H.

Hovsepian, S. Lory, Martin Blais, Hélène Manseau, Joanne Otis, and Marie-Eve Girard. "Prior Victimization and Sexual and Contraceptive Self-Efficacy among Adolescent Females under Child Protective Services Care." *Health Education & Behavior* 37, no. 1 (2010): 65–83, https://doi .org/10.1177/1090198108327730.

Kearns, Megan C., and Karen S. Calhoun. "Sexual Revictimization and Interpersonal Effectiveness." *Violence and Victims* 25, no. 4 (2010): 504–17, https://doi .org/10.1891/0886-6708.25.4.504.

Lamoureux, Brittain E., Patrick A. Palmieri, Anita P. Jackson, and Stevan E. Hobfoll. "Child Sexual Abuse and Adulthood-Interpersonal Outcomes: Examining Pathways for Intervention." *Psychological Trauma: Theory, Research, Practice, and Policy* 4, no. 6 (2011): 605–13, https://doi.org/10.1037/a0026079.

Lev-Wiesel, Rachel. "Quality of Life in Adult Survivors of Childhood Sexual Abuse Who Have Undergone Therapy." *Journal of Child Sexual Abuse* 9, no. 1 (2000): 1–13, https://doi.org/10.1300/J070v09n01_01.

Mercado, Roxanna, Alfonso Martínez-Taboas, and Orlando Pedrosa. "Childhood Sexual Abuse, Eating Disturbance and Dissociation: A Study in Puerto Rico." *Journal of Psychological Trauma* 7, no. 4 (2008): 298–309, https://doi.org/10.1080/19322880802266821.

Noll, Jennie G., Lisa A. Horowitz, George A. Bonanno, Penelope K. Trickett, and Frank W. Putnam. "Revictimization and Self-Harm in Females Who Experienced Childhood Sexual Abuse: Results from a Prospective Study." *Journal of Interpersonal Violence* 18, no. 12 (2003): 1452–71, https://doi.org/10.1177/0886260503258035.

O'Connor, Rory C., Susan Rasmussen, and Keith Hawton. "Predicting Deliberate Self-Harm in Adolescents: A Six Month Prospective Study." *Suicide and Life-Threatening Behavior* 39, no. 4 (2009): 364–75, https://doi.org/10.1521/suli.2009.39.4.364.

Reese-Weber, Marla, and Dana M. Smith. "Outcomes of Child Sexual Abuse as Predictors of Later Sexual Victimization."

Journal of Interpersonal Violence 26, no. 9 (2011): 1884–1905, https://doi.org/10.1177/0886260510372935.

Stern, Anne E., Deborah L. Lynch, R. Kim Oates, Brian I. O'Toole, and George Cooney. "Self Esteem, Depression, Behaviour and Family Functioning in Sexually Abused Children." *Journal of Child Psychology and Psychiatry* 36, no. 6 (1995): 1077–89, https://doi.org/10.1111/j.1469-7610.1995.tb01352.x.

Swanston, Heather Y., Angela M. Plunkett, Brian I. O'Toole, Sandra Shrimpton, Patrick N. Parkinson, and R. Kim Oates. "Nine Years After Child Sexual Abuse." *Child Abuse & Neglect* 27, no. 8 (2003): 967–84, https://doi.org/10.1016/S0145-2134(03)00143-1.

Printed in Great Britain
by Amazon

52233862R00151